Finance for the
Non-Financial Manager

E. B. Jones F.C.A., F.C.W.A., J.Dip.M.A.

 Pitman Publishing

First published 1972

SIR ISAAC PITMAN AND SONS LTD.
Pitman House, Parker Street, Kingsway, London, WC2B 5PB
P.O. Box 46038, Portal Street, Nairobi, Kenya

SIR ISAAC PITMAN (AUST.) PTY. LTD.
Pitman House, 158 Bouverie Street, Carlton, Victoria 3053, Australia

PITMAN PUBLISHING COMPANY S.A. LTD.
P.O Box 11231, Johannesburg, S. Africa

PITMAN PUBLISHING CORPORATION
6 East 43rd Street, New York, N.Y. 10017, U.S.A.

SIR ISAAC PITMAN (CANADA) LTD.
495 Wellington Street West, Toronto 135, Canada

THE COPP CLARK PUBLISHING COMPANY
517 Wellington Street, Toronto 135, Canada

ISBN: 0 273 36050 7

MADE IN GREAT BRITAIN AT THE PITMAN PRESS, BATH
G2—(TML 15:51)

Preface

Managers with no formal financial training or education are becoming increasingly curious about information presented to them by accountants. They feel it must be useful and for the first time they are beginning to question the need and use of each and every statement presented.

This is healthy to modern industry and commerce, but it is also a challenge to those presenting, and those being presented with, such data. Much has already been written about the different types of financial information, but such studies seem to be presented, in most cases, as a series of explanations of techniques rather than as a coherent account of their rationale.

This book is designed to overcome this difficulty by concentrating first upon the needs of non-financial managers at all levels for financial information and second to show the manner in which information has evolved in response to management's demands. As each technique is introduced emphasis is placed upon why the information is produced, and how it can be used by managers.

This concentration upon the needs of managers will involve tracing the development of financial information from its earliest stage to the modern sophistication of management accounting.

If the accountant is to justify his claim that he is a provider rather than a recorder of financial data his services must be used. This requires managers to be aware of this service and to demand its provision within his enterprise. It is the purpose of this book to assist this process and to make the provision of financial information subject more to the demands of management, and less to the whims of over- or under-zealous accountants.

Contents

1

The Development of Information

This book is primarily concerned with the financial information presented to managers—what is presented and how it is presented. However, before we discuss this in detail we should find out why any financial information is presented at all. If this can be explained it should assist the subsequent steps of understanding what it is and how it is presented.

In the first place it has to be conceded that businesses prospered before the introduction of modern sophisticated financial information systems. In fact, there is no correlation between the volume of financial information and prosperity. This may depress accountants, but it is none the less true. However, the provision of such information followed the demands of managers at all levels and its subsequent use has quite obviously greatly increased the efficiency and in its way the prosperity of many organizations. It is the demand for and use of data which are essential, and where these two vital aspects of financial information systems are lacking, the data presented will have decreasing value.

THE DEVELOPMENT OF FINANCIAL DATA

To see financial information in its true perspective, let us return to the beginning of financial investment in business. At that time the separation of the manager and the investor was unrealistic as he was the same person. Any attempt in those days to create a classification such as management accounting information would have been met with an incredulity which might be appropriate today.

In fact, in the early days the investor manager found he could arrive at the information he needed without any outside assistance

1

at all. This was financial information in its infancy, and it might be claimed to be an early example of "do it yourself" management control. It is nevertheless an interesting example of financial information, as the person providing the data must have really needed it and also must have used it. He was, after all, a busy man, and if he sacrificed his spare time to assemble information, it must have been important to him. And what were these vital financial data? Quite simply they were what everyone must know if he is making an investment or is responsible for supervising it.

THE INQUIRING MANAGER

Throughout this text we will refer to the inquiring manager seeking financial information but in each case for the word "manager" one can substitute "investor". The manager seeking financial information is trying to learn more about the investment under his control and these data are of equal interest to the investor. The present split of such information into that appropriate to management, as opposed to others, has been brought about more because of limitations on financial data thought desirable when presented to investors, i.e. shareholders of limited companies, than on account of any real division of requirements. It could be argued that any inquiring investor would be very happy to receive the data at present classified as appropriate to managers, and would perhaps be more likely to use them!

The Business Investment

To illustrate the investment aspect of business, we shall examine the flow of money in a manufacturing business diagrammatically.

In the case of a non-manufacturing organization the diagram would be revised to exclude finished goods and it should be noted that, if a business decides to invest outside itself, this would be shown as an additional ball representing such investments. To illustrate this we show below the flow of money for a non-manufacturing business which has some outside investments.

It should be understood that these diagrams are equally valid whether we are describing a business of enormous size and complexity or one which is small and without complication.

THE KEY DIAGRAMS

We shall use these diagrams to illustrate business investment and to trace the development of information for both managers and

2

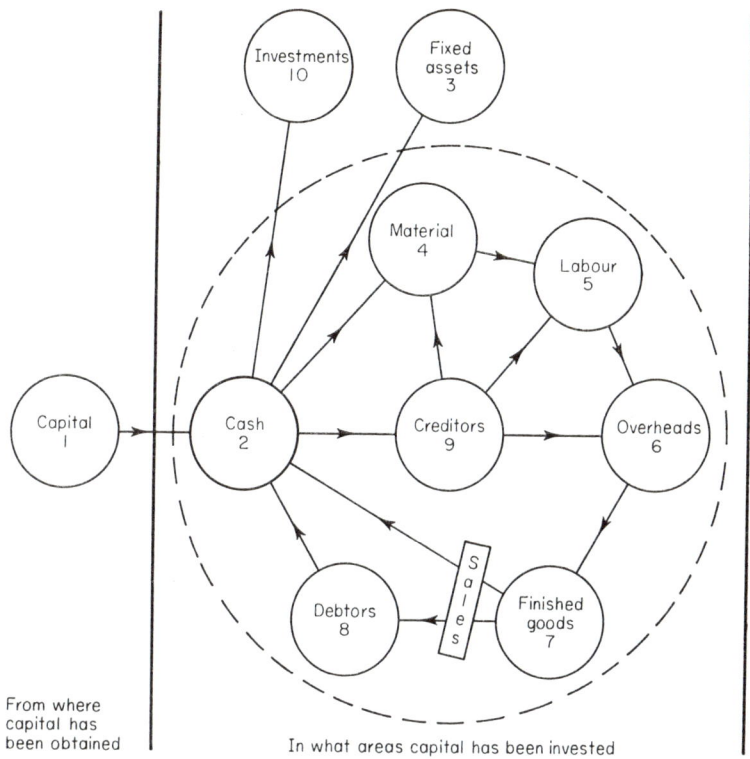

From where
capital has
been obtained

In what areas capital has been invested

FIGURE 1 Key diagram—Manufacturing business

investors throughout the text of this book. We shall begin by explaining each item.

Capital

The diagram sets out the two aspects of investment which require understanding, namely from where capital has been obtained and in what areas it has been invested.

The capital circle relates to the first aspect and is concerned with the sources of permanent capital invested within the business. It should be recognized that temporary capital may be obtained by means of a bank overdraft or by extending the time taken before paying for goods or services, but when describing capital in its long-term context we refer to two main sources, namely the owner's own capital and loans of a permanent nature. An example of these

3

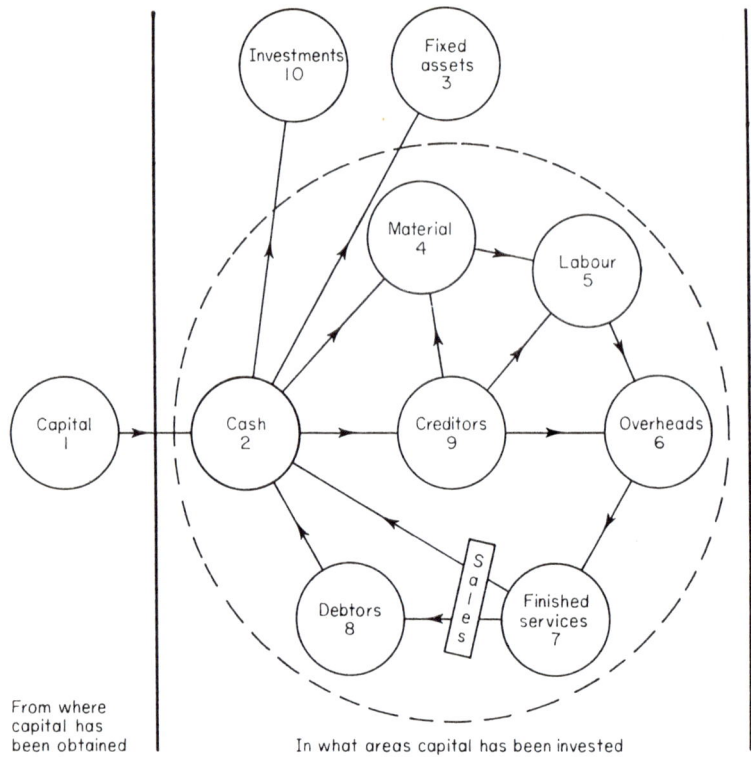

In what areas capital has been invested

FIGURE 2 **Key diagram—Non-manufacturing business**

sources in a small business would be, first, the money obtained from the proprietor himself and, second, that obtained by a loan from his mother-in-law. In the case of a large public company we would substitute for these two items share capital and debenture capital. It is emphasized that when referring to the capital of the organization we are defining the sources of capital and not the areas in which it has been invested.

Cash

For convenience it is assumed that all capital will originally enter the business in the form of cash. This, of course, may not be so if, for example, a business is started and the proprietor already owns a property which he uses as his shop or factory premises. However, the introduction of this property simply avoids the need of converting cash into this item and so, if we assume cash as the starting point, it will be logical and will in no way over-simplify the real-life situation.

The Investment Division

Capital in its original form is cash and the investor/manager is faced with the primary investment problem, "What shall I spend it on?" A list of the items on which money must be spent in a business irrespective of its nature would include the following: premises, shop or factory, raw materials, wages, plant and machinery or shopfittings, land, salaries, rent, motor vehicles, advertising, rates, etc.

It will be found that each item listed above falls into one or other of the two main categories of business investment, namely items not bought for sale, e.g. land, premises, plant and machinery, motor vehicles and shop fittings, and items bought specifically for sale or conversion into a saleable product or service, e.g. raw material, wages, salaries, rent, advertising and sales.

This division of the investment is the first step that must be taken by every businessman, and it is not a "once and for all" decision. It is a continuous decision process. Once a business is established fresh capital will be introduced and in its raw state of cash will require decisions to be made as to the areas in which it should be invested. A decision will also be required when a change in investment takes place, such as when some plant and machinery is sold and the resultant new cash is then available for reinvestment.

Fixed Assets

It will be seen that cash may be spent on items which are not for resale but which are used to further the trade of the business. The items which make up this area are referred to as fixed assets, appearing as circle 3 in the key diagram. Their classification as fixed assets will depend upon the business and will be determined by the purpose for which the items were purchased. In financial information several names are given to the same items and, in the case of fixed assets, these are often referred to as capital expenditure. The use of this latter term is of special relevance when dealing with business taxation and is probably the reason for its adoption when referring to fixed assets.

The duplication of terms and the lack of precise definition is a continuous difficulty to those wishing to understand accounting information, and every effort should be made to clarify a context to those unversed in financial jargon and expression.

Working Capital

The second class of items invested in any business consists of those which are purchased with the specific intention of their resale or conversion into a saleable product or service, and this investment is termed collectively "working capital". It is a net investment, and to refer back to the key diagram includes material, labour and overheads, stored prior to sale in the three stock forms of raw material, work in progress or process and finished goods. The types of stock held will depend upon the nature of the business. Thus a retail grocer will have only one type of stock, viz. raw material goods, whereas a furniture manufacturer would hold all three types of stock, viz. raw material, work in progress and finished goods.

Also contained in working capital will be the amount locked up in people who have not paid for goods when credit sales take place. People who buy goods on normal trade credit terms are referred to as debtors or accounts receivable. In addition to this item there may be sums of cash uninvested but available for any contingency which may arise. The total of the stock plus debtors and surplus cash may be termed the gross working capital but this must be reduced by the value of material, labour and overheads—rent, rates, telephone, salaries, which have not been paid for. Those who are owed money by the business in this way are termed creditors or accounts payable and are shown as item 9 on the key diagram.

The net amount computed in this manner is known as the working capital and is the money required to support the sales of the business. The volume of this investment will depend upon how speedily material, labour and overheads can be converted back into cash and to some extent how long people can be persuaded to wait for money due to them. The control of this investment is therefore a question of time control. It should be noted at this stage that the lower the working capital investment is per £ of sales, the more sales can be increased without the need for more permanent investment in this area. If it can be reduced to nil, sales expansion will be permanently limited only by fixed assets, capacity to produce or shelve the goods or services for sale and/or the saleability of the goods themselves. This investment could therefore be called the spring-board for business expansion.

Outside Investments

As mentioned earlier in this chapter, there is a third area in which capital may be invested, and that is outside investment. This area is normally associated with the large public corporations, but it is in fact available to any business which has funds free for investment and sees advantages in using them in this way. Examples of these advantages are that such investment might produce a superior return or that it might provide a spread and therefore a reduction in the investment risk.

General

This, therefore, is the explanation of the key diagram and it should now be possible to discuss the movement of business investment without recourse to jargon or over-technical expressions.

EVOLUTION OF INFORMATION

Now let us consider what information everyone requires if he makes an investment or is responsible for its supervision. In other words what does the investor or manager require regularly to know about the funds invested in the business? The answer to this question is exactly the same information as is required about all investment by anyone concerned with it which is:

1 Where is the investment? and
2 How has it grown during a given period of time?

All financial information systems start by answering these two fundamental questions and the development of the different information techniques can be seen as a natural evolution from the answers provided to them. We shall now examine these two questions and the answers sought by those concerned with business.

Where Is the Investment?

This question is often assumed by the manager to be too obvious to ask, but in fact it is fundamental to all investment problems and in the business context, as in all others, the disposition of funds will dictate all financial progress.

The main feature about business investment which makes it different from other investment, such as that in land or stocks and shares and jewellery, is its fluidity. The investment is continually changing its form. In the case of working capital the investment is flowing between material and cash with a hesitation in the middle to account for creditors, and the speedier and, as previously explained, the more changing this investment is, the better. Also in the case of fixed assets, although more stability can be expected,

7

by accountants to such comparisons. The important point to understand in this situation is that accounting and the information presented is a service to the investor and manager and that it was created to meet a very real demand. This service aspect of financial information reinforces the need for both demand and use to be present before its provision.

PROFIT AND LOSS STATEMENTS AND BALANCE SHEETS

We shall now examine the profit and loss statement and the balance sheet separately and trace how, from these two information foundations, has stemmed all other financial data. In each case we shall see how demand and use have grown from previous information supplied and how each information technique is created in response to the progressive demands of managers in an increasingly sophisticated business setting.

Profit and Loss Statement

This statement summarizes the expenses against income for any selected time span, taking care to carry forward expenses which are not reflected in the income for the period—for example stock.
 A profit and loss statement is illustrated below:

A LIMITED

PROFIT AND LOSS STATEMENT

For the Period Ended 31 March 19..

	£		£
Materials	60,000	Sales	140,000
Labour	30,000	Investment Interest . .	10,000
Factory Expenses . .	10,000		
Administration Expenses .	6,000		
Selling Expenses . . .	11,000		
Distribution Expenses . .	4,000		
Financial Expenses . .	3,000		
Net Profit	26,000		
	150,000		150,000

This right- and left-hand side presentation which takes the form of an account is not sacred in any way and the information can quite easily be presented in a vertical form, as follows:

10

A LIMITED
PROFIT AND LOSS STATEMENT
For the Period Ended 31 March 19..

		£
Sales		140,000
Investment Income		10,000
		150,000

	£	
LESS: Materials	60,000	
Labour	30,000	
Factory Expenses	10,000	
Administration Expenses	6,000	
Selling Expenses	11,000	
Distribution Expenses	4,000	
Financial Expenses	3,000	
		124,000
Net Profit		26,000

(It should be especially noted that the net profit or net loss for a period is the difference between expenses and income).

The manner of presentation depends upon the requirements of those receiving the data and it is the duty of the presenter to market his goods, that is the information, to suit their needs. In whatever form the information may be presented, the profit and loss statement is one half of the manager's information needs. It is the statement which shows the investment's growth from the trading activities of the enterprise, and the profit or loss becomes the measure of return on the capital employed.

Developments from the Profit and Loss Statement

Because this statement shows the return of the enterprise it will be studied with great care by anyone concerned with investment. From any such study it will become apparent that the return or result (profit or loss) shown is net for the period concerned. It is therefore impossible to determine, first, where precisely the return was made and, second if more than one product or service is produced by the business, exactly how much of the return refers to one product or service, as opposed to another.

Frequency of Presentation

To illustrate the first difficulty, let us consider a profit and loss statement prepared for a twelve-month period and showing a net

11

profit of £480,000. From this information it is impossible to tell whether this profit was made equally over the whole period—that is £40,000 per month—or whether the majority of the profit occurred in the first half of the year, or even that for the last three months there has been a loss. After all, the profit is net and the statement cannot provide the answers to these very real questions which any inquiring manager would wish to have. To assist in answering this problem it has become usual for managers to request more frequent profit and loss statement presentation and it is now quite common to find such statements quarterly, and monthly presentation is not unusual. It is stressed that this demand for frequency flows from an inquiring manager's mind without any promptings from legal requirements.

Analysis of Data

The second problem, that of finding out exactly where the profit or loss has occurred, is the next information demand area. Having had supplied to him more frequent profit and loss statements the manager is still faced with the problem of knowing exactly where such profit or loss has occurred if we assume his business is concerned with producing more than one product or service. The need will therefore express itself by the manager turning towards the person concerned with presenting financial information and asking for a breakdown of the net profit or loss. The system which will be used to answer this demand will be one which will analyse the material, labour and other expenses and the sales income under the several products or services of the enterprise. Such analysis will lead to the required breakdown of the profit or loss for any period, and the system used is known as "costing."

Costing is based on very careful analysis and control so that the information is of real and practical value to management. The data on page 13 are set out to illustrate the way in which costs are presented for a series of manufactured products.

It will be noted that the expenses are divided between those which can be traced directly to the product and are termed "direct" and those which have to be apportioned on some equitable basis over all the products, and these are known as "indirect" expenses. Both these terms will be examined in detail in Chapter 3.

The importance for management to recognize the need for accurate analysis is also dealt with in Chapter 3, but at this stage it is stressed that the total of the analysis must be agreed back with the main items in the profit and loss statement. For example, the materials amount to 35p plus 40p plus 25p plus 30p and plus all the other

| | PRODUCTS | | | |
| | A | B | C | D |
	£	£	£	£
Direct Material	0·35	0·40	0·25	0·30
Direct Labour	0·20	0·25	0·10	0·20
Direct Expenses	0·10	0·05	0·15	0·05
Prime Cost	0·65	0·70	0·50	0·55
INDIRECT EXPENSES:				
Works	0·40	0·30	0·25	0·35
Works Cost	1·05	1·00	0·75	0·90
Administration	0·30	0·25	0·20	0·20
Cost of Production	1·35	1·25	0·95	1·10
Selling	0·60	0·90	0·20	0·40
Distribution	0·25	0·20	0·15	0·20
Cost of Sales	2·20	2·35	1·30	1·70
Net Profit/Loss	0·30	0·25	0·40	−0·20
Sales Price	2·50	2·60	1·70	1·50

material costs contained in each product costed during the period
and must be agreed back to the profit and loss statement for the
period. If this analysis is referred to A Limited, set out in the profit
and loss statement illustration, these items should total £60,000.

This total control is vital as well as the need to make sure that the
right expense and revenue have been analysed to the appropriate
product or service. If such control is absent there may be a large
amount of expense or income unallocated to any product or service,
so that what appears to be a profitable business from the cost
information may turn out to be unprofitable once the profit and
loss statement for the relevant period is prepared.

Cost Comparison

This additional demand for the analysis of profit or loss, which
heralds the introduction of a costing system, is a major step in the
provision of financial information. It is also from the costing data
that the next information demand may often arise.

To understand this next stage let us examine a cost as set out in
the previous illustration and ask ourselves: If we were supplied
with such data would this be sufficient or would we find it even more
useful with something else? It is suggested that this "something else"
would be a comparison. A comparison with the estimate of the cost

might be a starting point but this would evolve into trying to find a comparison with a target based on whatever level of efficiency is desired and this could be used as a measure against the actual costs.

This search for comparison would therefore lead to the preparation of costs showing actual and target or budget expenses and income for each product at source as is set out below:

PRODUCT A

	Actual £	Budget £	Difference £
Direct Material	0·50	0·45	+0·05
Direct Labour	0·30	0·35	−0·05
Direct Expenses	0·10	0·15	−0·05
Prime Cost	0·90	0·95	−0·05
INDIRECT EXPENSES:			
Works Expenses	0·35	0·40	−0·05
Works Cost	1·25	1·35	−0·10
Administration Expenses	0·20	0·20	—
Cost of Production	1·45	1·55	−0·10
Selling Expenses	0·60	0·55	+0·05
Distribution Expenses	0·15	0·15	—
Cost of Sales	2·20	2·25	−0·05
Net Profit/Loss	0·30	0·35	−0·05
Sales Price	2·50	2·60	−0·10

Standard Costing

At this stage it might be felt that the inquiring manager has gone far enough in his search for amplification of the profit and loss statement, but in practice he is found to be still unsatisfied. He finds that, despite the fact that the comparative data throw out a difference under each head between the actual and a pre-established target or budget, such differences require further analysis if effective action is to be taken. To illustrate this dilemma consider the difference between actual and budget. The purpose of this difference column is to enable the manager to take positive action to prevent bad differences recurring and to see whether good differences can be made to continue. However, before any such action can be taken it is necessary to pinpoint the causes of the difference and this requires further investigation. For example, in the case of material, the cause could be the price of the material used. The actual material

14

used could have cost more or less than the budget. Or again the difference could have been caused because more or less material in quantity was used than specified in the budget or it could be a combination of both these reasons. In the case of labour it could be the rate of pay or the time required to produce a service.

However complex this analysis may be, it is vital if managers are to locate precisely where the responsibility lies for not achieving the target set. For this reason the inquiring manager demands a method of comparison which separates the differences into their several causes as soon as they arise without having to wait for time-wasting post-mortems on net difference figures. To answer this demand a system known as *standard costing* has been devised, which not only compares actual costs with pre-set targets, but simultaneously divides the differences under each expense and income head into their separate causes. These cause sub-differences are known as variances.

The volume and extent of the comparison technique and variance analysis will depend upon the needs of managers and these must be carefully selected when providing this detailed information service. It must always be remembered that financial information can only be provided at a cost, and therefore there must exist both a demand and use for it.

General

These, therefore, are the information techniques that have grown from the profit and loss statement. Each has developed from the other and each owes its existence to the inquiring manager who wishes to improve his control and supervision of the return on the capital employed in the business.

THE BALANCE SHEET

We shall now trace the development of information from the other main financial statement, namely the balance sheet, but before we proceed we shall first examine this basic statement.

The balance sheet sets out the two aspects of business investment. These are, first, the area or areas from which the money—that is capital—has been obtained and, second, the areas in which it has been placed—that is invested. If we refer back to the key diagram, the balance sheet is a snapshot of this in financial terms. To illustrate this situation, let us examine a balance sheet presented for a medium-sized company, and then present the same information in the form of a key diagram:

A LIMITED

BALANCE SHEET

as at 31 March 19..

	£				£
Share Capital . . .	5,000	FIXED ASSETS:			
Reserves	4,000	Property			5,000
Long-term Loans . .	1,000	Plant & Machinery . .			3,000
	———	Office Equipment . .			1,000
	10,000				———
					9,000
		Investment . . .			500
CURRENT LIABILITIES:				£	
Creditors	3,450	CURRENT ASSETS:			
		Stocks: Raw Materials	400		
		Stocks: Work in Pro-			
		gress . .	1,200		
		Stocks: Finished			
		Goods .	1,300		
		Debtors . .	1,000		
		Bank & Cash .	50		
				———	3,950
	———				———
	£13,450				£13,450

The key diagram (Fig. 3, page 17) sets out the values against each item in its circle and these can be traced back to the balance sheet statement. In the case of work in progress it should be understood that the amount of £1,200 is made up of the cost of material, labour and other expenses contained in partly finished goods in the process of manufacture.

It should be noted that the balance sheet presented above is one which owes its form more to the convenience of the presenter of information than to the needs of the inquiring manager. In recent years these statements have been adapted to the real needs of those wishing to learn about the particular businesses and an example of how the same information might be presented more clearly is set out on page 18.

GENERAL

The balance sheet is a statement of investment as at any particular point in time, unlike a profit and loss statement which is *for* a period of time. The second illustration of the balance sheet sets out each area of investment, namely fixed assets, investments and working

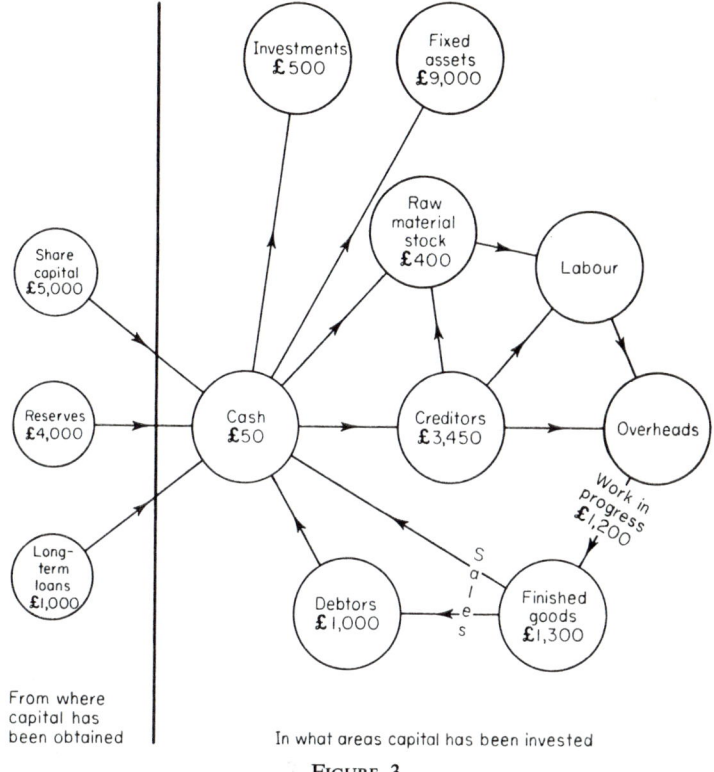

Investments £500

Fixed assets £9,000

Raw material stock £400

Labour

Share capital £5,000

Reserves £4,000

Cash £50

Creditors £3,450

Overheads

Long-term loans £1,000

Debtors £1,000

Sales

Finished goods £1,300

Work in progress £1,200

From where capital has been obtained

In what areas capital has been invested

FIGURE 3

capital, and follows this by defining the areas from which it has been obtained, namely share capital, reserves and long-term loans.

It could be argued that a balance sheet is a very honest statement as few people, if asked to describe their wealth, would go so far as to reveal not just what they own but also how they had obtained the money to own it in the first place!

Presentation

Presentation is certainly as important for balance sheets as profit and loss statements, and it is most necessary that those receiving the data should ask for clarification if they need it. This should include clarity of presentation as much as subject matter, as one can quite easily influence the other.

A rule which can be applied by those presented with data, as to whether or not they fulfil their purpose in this respect, is to see

17

A LIMITED
Balance Sheet
As at 31 March 19..

	£	£
Fixed Assets:		
Property	5,000	
Plant & Machinery	3,000	
Office Equipment	1,000	
		9,000
Investments		500
Working Capital:		
Current Assets	£	
Stocks: Raw Material . . .	400	
Work in Progress . . .	1,200	
Finished Goods . . .	1,300	
Debtors	1,000	
Bank and Cash	50	
	3,950	
Less Current Liability:		
Creditors	3,450	
		500
		£10,000
Financed by:		
Share Capital		5,000
Reserves		4,000
Long-term Loans		1,000
		£10,000

whether the main information is clearly seen without further calculation or data manipulation. Thus, in the case of a balance sheet, it should be possible to see where capital is invested under the three heads, fixed assets, investment and working capital, and also the main areas from which such capital has been obtained, namely proprietors' capital, retained profits and long-term loans.

Developments of Information from the Balance Sheet

The balance sheet is the primary source of information on investment within any enterprise. It sets out exactly where capital is employed and the success or failure of the business will depend to a large extent upon the way in which such investment is made and used. For this reason the balance sheet contains the key data for both managers and investors and the more senior the management the more important the data become.

FREQUENCY

The development of information from this primary document initially follows that which has already been described for profit and loss statements. The first demand is again for more frequency, but in the case of balance sheets, it is not because the information presented is net, but in order to have a measure against which to review the profit or the loss for the period. This is to determine the capital employed on which the return has been made. The second reason for frequent balance sheets is to review the investment so that changes can be seen and their effect on profit measured.

INVESTMENT PLANNING

The fluidity of investment within a business, already mentioned, is such that constant review is vital if changes in investment are to be satisfactorily controlled and identified. To fulfil this function properly, it is necessary to do more than review what has happened by producing a balance sheet as at any point in time. It is also necessary to plan exactly when the capital should be invested and the source from which it will be obtained. This calls for overall planning in the form of budgetary control. This information technique is one which embraces both the balance sheet and profit and loss statement, and is referred to later in this chapter.

FIXED ASSET APPRAISAL

The information techniques which develop solely from balance sheets are those which stem from an inquiring manager wishing more fully to use the basic investment information. To understand this need we must first study and understand the data presented in the balance sheet. From such study and understanding it will be found that a balance sheet is a summary of investment. It will also be found that every manager is judged financially by the rate of return on the capital employed within his control. For this reason every manager wishes to maximize the return on investment. He will realize that, like investment in any other field, it is preferable to assess what the return is likely to be before making it, so as not to be disappointed by further events.

It is therefore quite natural that, when investment is to be made permanently with no intention of sale, that is in fixed assets, an inquiring manager will ask for information which will assist in his decisions in this area. To meet this request several techniques have been developed to assist the manager and these are dealt with in detail in Chapter 5, under the title Investment Appraisal Techniques.

In addition to fixed assets money may be invested in working capital. As explained earlier in this chapter, the object of this area of investment is to maximize the sales or turnover that can be obtained from each unit of capital. This maximization enables a business to expand its sales to the limit of its fixed asset capacity and/or the saleability of its goods or services without the constant fear of outstripping its working capital resources. The technique developed to assist the manager in this area, dealt with in detail in Chapter 6, is known as working capital analysis, and is concerned with an examination of the key factor in this area of investment time.

JOINT INFORMATION TECHNIQUES

These two techniques complete the information developed from the balance sheet to assist managers in their control and supervision of investment, but there are several joint techniques which stem from both the balance sheet and the profit and loss statement.

Budgetary Control

The first of these joint techniques which has been referred to in respect of both profit and loss statements and balance sheets is *budgetary control*. It is difficult to imagine anyone who wishes to manage a business enterprise not first setting out his plans. As soon as these become translated into financial terms one has a budget.

Budgetary control is the discipline demanded by all thoughtful managers of first subjecting their dreams and schemes to financial translation in whatever form the manager feels useful, and then comparing the actual results with these forecasts. This subject is dealt with in considerable detail in Chapter 4, but at present it should be noted that, although budgetary control will be presented in its final form as a budgeted profit and loss statement and balance sheet, there is a paramount need to express budgets in terms of the expense and income within each manager's span of control. For this reason a manager who demands and wishes to use this information technique must take an active part in its development so that the data are presented relevantly.

Cash and Fund Flow Analysis

The second item of information flowing from both the profit and loss statement and the balance sheet, and which is becoming more and more generally sought after by managers, is the technique known as *cash and fund flow analysis*. This technique is concerned with summarizing the changes in sources of capital employed within the enterprise and marrying these up with the several investment areas.

It has very special concern for the investor wishing to review the stewardship of the directors, as a review of cash and fund flow within an enterprise will show the logic or otherwise of the investment decisions made by its management. For this reason, management is well advised to become familiar with this technique, which is presented in detail in a later chapter.

Final Account Interpretation

The last of these joint techniques is concerned with the interpretation of profit and loss statements and balance sheets. To assist in this work the technique of ratio analysis is available, and this will be discussed at a later stage, together with comparative information sources from such bodies as Interfirm Comparison Ltd. It must, however, be noted that the most important technique of all to assist in interpreting financial data is understanding and an ability to ask why.

GENERAL

It is vital for all managers to become aware of financial information and to demand its presentation so as to meet their need to control and manage the business investment, but once this has been done the data must be used. It is hoped that this chapter has shown how each piece of financial information has been developed and how each flows logically, from the other, stemming from either the profit and loss statement or balance sheet or both.

It is also stressed that the motivating force in presenting such information has been the inquiring manager, who should always be the catalyst in the development of such data. For this reason it is most necessary for management to use the accountancy service which is available within the organization.

Such use will include asking for data which are felt to be useful and demanding the presentation of such data in a manner which can be readily understood. By taking an active part in developing this information service, management will greatly assist its effectiveness. But it will be the way in which the data are used which will ultimately determine whether or not the cost is justified.

2 *The Profit and Loss Statement and Balance Sheet*

The previous chapter pointed out that all financial information starts from the profit and loss account and balance sheet. These two statements, often referred to as the final accounts of a business, are the information foundation upon which all else is built. It has become fashionable to concentrate upon the derivative techniques such as marginal costing and discounted cash flow, but we shall try to reverse this trend and give due emphasis to these two primary documents.

ACCURACY AND SPEED OF PRESENTATION

The paramount need for verifying return on capital employed makes continuous presentation of profit and loss statements and balance sheets essential. However, for such data to be of real use to management, they must be made available as soon as possible after the date of the final accounts. To decide the speed of presentation two, at times conflicting, considerations are necessary. The first is accuracy and the second is understanding that the data presented long after their due date become, in many cases, valueless, except for general interest.

It is vital that managers seeking up-to-date presentation should be aware of these two considerations as they can, in many cases, affect each other. A high degree of accuracy in the information is important as inaccurate data could be at best misleading and at worst damaging. At the same time total accuracy, if that is possible at all, will delay presentation and this may lead to data appearing too long after the events set out, and thus becoming totally irrelevant. The reconciliation of this dilemma of accuracy versus speed is one which occurs in the presentation of all information and becomes very apparent in the case of final accounts.

This is not a problem which management can delegate to the information service, i.e. the accountancy function. All managers who receive information must recognize the problem and set down specifically their policy on these matters. This policy will vary from one area of information to another, but a clear policy will greatly assist the preparation of financial data.

UNDERSTANDING THE PRODUCTION PROCEDURE

The temptation to delegate decisions such as that outlined above also occurs in the understanding of how the profit and loss statement and balance sheet are prepared. It is believed by many managers that the technical side of preparation can be safely left to those concerned with the production of the information. This appears to be a logical approach leaving the detail to the experts and reserving to management the duty of reviewing the final statements presented. However, this approach ignores the fact that the presentation of information is a service and the final product is vital to both managers and investors. If such information is delayed it affects managers, as decisions may either have to be postponed or made without the aid of such data. For this reason, it is necessary for managers to be aware of the processes required to produce the information.

Such knowledge will enable them to question delays and to discuss bottlenecks in the presentation of data without depending entirely upon the explanations of those concerned with their production. This need to understand the production processes is similar to the need of a salesman to know how the product he sells is produced. It provides the manager with a deeper understanding of the information presented. This should lead to a far greater ability to interpret the data than is normally found among managers, as well as the knowledge with which to question delays and to suggest ways and means of overcoming difficulties.

RECORDING FINANCIAL TRANSACTIONS

General

It would be wrong to suggest that all managers should have the ability to record financial transactions and also be able to prepare final accounts. It is, however, essential for all managers to know that in order to prepare final accounts, financial transactions must be recorded. Such recording can be undertaken by quill pen or computer, but the end result will be identical—all financial transactions will be recorded.

Double-entry Book-keeping

The second point about recording which should be known by all managers is that, whatever means of recording is adopted, the method will involve what some might refer to as duality and others as double-entry book-keeping. However it may be described it implies that each financial transaction has two aspects, both of which are of interest to managers, and both of which are recorded. For example, the introduction by the proprietor of £100,000 into his business in the form of cash will be recorded to show £100,000 owing to the proprietor and £100,000 held by the business in the form of cash. As cash is expended on various items, so each will be recorded and cash will be reduced.

Throughout this system, double recording is made in such a manner as to enable one aspect of the transaction to be recorded on the left-hand side and the other on the right-hand side in what are termed accounts. In the case of computer applications, entries are given positive or negative ratings. Left-hand side and positive entries are termed debits and right-hand side and negative entries credits. It is hoped that this jargon will not depress the reader too much. It has been found that people approaching this subject for the first time find difficulty in the terms debit and credit, as their only knowledge of these forms comes from bank statements. These have often rather an emotional connotation in that debits or overdrafts are bad and credits or cash in hand are good. Such feelings should be suppressed in viewing the system of recording financial transactions and it is hoped the following illustration may help in this respect.

Example of Double Entry

The following transactions take place during the month of January 19.. in the business of A Ltd.

					£
(1) Capital received in cash from shareholders	.	.	.	.	100,000
(2) Plant and machinery purchased for cash	.	.	.	.	20,000
(3) Freehold factory ,, ,, ,,	.	.	.	.	30,000
(4) Leasehold office ,, ,, ,,	.	.	.	.	10,000
(5) Raw material ,, ,, ,,	.	.	.	.	20,000
(6) Raw material purchased from B Ltd	.	.	.	.	5,000

		£
(7) Wages paid	. . . .	8,000
(8) Rent paid	. . . .	1,000
(9) Rates paid	. . . .	200
(10) Insurance paid	. . . .	3,000
(11) Paid B Ltd for material	. . . . . .	5,000
(12) Car sales	. . . .	10,000
(13) Sale of goods to C Ltd	. . . . . .	2,000
(14) Received amount due from C Ltd .	. . . . .	—
(15) Sale of goods to D & Co.	. . . . . .	750

SHARE CAPITAL ACCOUNT

		£			£
Jan Balance b/d	. .	100,000	Jan Cash (1)	. . .	100,000
		100,000			100,000
			Jan Balance c/d	. .	100,000

CASH ACCOUNT

		£			£
Jan Capital (1)	. .	100,000	Jan Plant & Machinery (2) .		20,000
Sales (12)	. . .	10,000	Freehold Factory (3)	.	30,000
C Ltd (14)	. . .	2,000	Leasehold Office (4)	.	10,000
			Raw Material (5)	.	20,000
			Wages (7)	. . .	8,000
			Rent (8)	. . .	1,000
			Rates (9)	. . .	200
			Insurance (10)	. .	3,000
			B Ltd (11)	. . .	5,000
			*Balance c/d	. .	14,800
		112,000			112,000
Balance b/d	. . .	14,800			

PLANT AND MACHINERY ACCOUNT

Jan Cash (2)	. . .	20,000	Jan Balance c/d	. .	20,000
		20,000			20,000
Jan Balance b/d	. .	20,000			

FREEHOLD FACTORY ACCOUNT

Jan Cash (3)	. . .	30,000	Jan Balance c/d	. .	30,000
		30,000			30,000
Jan Balance b/d	. .	30,000			

*c/d = Carried Down
b/d = Brought Down

25

Leasehold Office Account

	£			£
Jan Cash (4) . . .	10,000	Jan Balance c/d . .		10,000
	10,000			10,000
Jan Balance b/d . .	10,000			

Raw Material Account

	£			£
Jan Cash (5) . . .	20,000	Jan Balance c/d . .		25,000
B Ltd. . . .	5,000			
	25,000			25,000
Jan Balance b/d . .	25,000			

Wages Account

	£			£
Jan Cash (7) . . .	8,000	Jan Balance c/d . .		8,000
	8,000			8,000
Jan Balance b/d . .	8,000			

Rent Account

	£			£
Jan Cash (8) . . .	1,000	Jan Balance c/d . .		1,000
	1,000			1,000
Jan Balance b/d . .	1,000			

Rates

	£			£
Jan Cash (9) . . .	200	Jan Balance c/d . .		200
	200			200
Jan Balance b/d . .	200			

Insurance

	£			£
Jan Cash (10) . . .	3,000	Jan Balance c/d . .		3,000
	3,000			3,000
Jan Balance b/d . .	3,000			

B Ltd

	£			£
Jan Cash (11) . . .	5,000	Jan Raw Materials (6) .		5,000

SALES ACCOUNT

	£				£
Jan Balance c/d. . .	12,750	Jan Cash (12) .	.	.	10,000
		C Ltd (13) .	.	.	2,000
		D & Co. (15)			750
	12,750				12,750
		Jan Balance b/d	.	.	12,750

C Ltd

Jan Sales (13) . . .	2,000	Jan Cash (14) .	.	.	2,000

D & Co.

Jan Sales (15) . . .	750	Jan Balance c/d	.	. 750
	750			750
Jan Balance b/d . .	750			

Need for Analysis

Special note should be made of the fact that the number, and there-fore the volume, of recordings will be determined by the demands of management for analysis. If management requires to know the investment in plant and machinery as opposed to freehold property, separate accounts will be required for each item and this is equally true for such expenses as rent, rates, insurance and wages.

The need for analysis in this way will be determined by management, and managers should be aware that the more analysis required the more onerous will be the recording task. However limited the analysis may be, the volume of transactions to be recorded even in a medium-sized concern is such that considerable delay can be caused in the presentation of final accounts unless recording is kept well up to date. This will ensure that at the date when a profit and loss statement and balance sheet is to be presented there will be no delay caused by the need to record a mass of financial transactions which have been left unentered. For this reason it is vital that such trans-actions are entered on a daily basis.

Trial Balance

The double-entry recording makes possible an arithmetic check on the transactions known as a trial balance. This is simply a summary of the accounts in which the financial transactions have been recorded. In order to summarize an account the difference between the left- and right-hand side is calculated, which is termed the balance of the account, and if the left-hand or debit balances are added together they should equal the sum of right-hand or credit balances. In the case of computers, the positive minus the negative items should equal nil. To illustrate this point the trial balance of the accounts set out in the previous illustration is given below:

A LTD

TRIAL BALANCE

as at 31 March 19. .

	Debit £	Credit £
Share capital		100,000
Cash	14,800	
Plant and Machinery	20,000	
Freehold Factory	30,000	
Leasehold Office	10,000	
Raw Materials	25,000	
Wages	8,000	
Rent	1,000	
Rates	200	
Insurance	3,000	
Sales		12,750
D & Co.	750	
	£112,750	£112,750

It should be noted that a trial balance agreement is essential before proceeding to the preparation of final accounts, as it establishes the necessary arithmetic check on the recording of the underlying transactions. If immediate agreement does not take place, it will be necessary to check the recordings and verify the double entry for each transaction. This is a cumbersome task, which delays the final account preparation. For this reason it is vital that, however infrequently profit and loss statements and balance sheets are prepared, the trial balance should be agreed at least monthly if recording by conventional methods, and if by computer each batch of data should be agreed in batch lots. The trial balance can be likened to a final inspection of a production process, and in both cases disagreement has a severe effect upon the time of presentation of the final result.

THE PREPARATION OF FINAL ACCOUNTS:
THE MECHANICS
General

The time it takes to prepare and present final accounts is therefore affected by the following:

(i) the volume of entries to be recorded at the date at which the final accounts are to be presented;

(ii) the volume of analysis required by management which will in turn affect the number of accounts which will require opening;

(iii) the time it takes to agree the trial balance, which will be influenced first by the accuracy of the recording and second by the frequency of agreement.

The mechanics of recording are often presumed to be outside the concern of managers, but it is difficult to reconcile this with the accepted need for management to receive such financial information as speedily as possible. It is hardly possible for the manager to assess the speed or otherwise of the presentation unless he is able to examine the reasons for delay offered by the presenter of information. It is suggested that, unless managers are able to understand the reasons given, it is unlikely that those responsible are going to admit their own fault in this respect.

Adjustments

We have now examined the recording procedures which form the background of account preparation, but there is still a further step that must be taken before the profit and loss statement and balance sheet can be prepared. This is the task of preparing what is termed "the adjustments."

The recording technique and the arithmetic check accomplished through a trial balance have indeed been examined, but the purpose of this information production cycle is to present final accounts. The adjustments are the final vital step which bridges the gap between the trial balance and the presented profit and loss account and balance sheet. They are required to take care of the following circumstances which arise in the construction of these statements.

PREPAYMENTS AND ACCRUALS

These strange-sounding names refer to the need to adjust expenses recorded in the accounts, so as to bring them into line with the period covered by the profit and loss statement and the date of the balance sheet.

These adjustments are necessary as the expenses recorded in the accounts will be those which have been paid for by cash or for which invoices have been received during the period without any reference as to whether they relate exactly to the period or not. A prepayment refers to a recorded expense which refers wholly or in part to a period beyond that for which the final accounts are being presented, and in the reverse situation an accrual will be required.

Accruals and prepayments can be seen by examining what has been recorded at the date of the trial balance and asking oneself if this is the full amount of expense for the period. It will be necessary to be especially careful to examine such items as wages to see that what is recorded covers the full period under review, or whether the next wage payment in the following period should be brought partly into account. This is equally true for materials supplied at the close of any period. Care must be taken to ensure that the invoice for these materials has been recorded and, if not, the necessary accrual must be made.

We shall now examine an illustration setting out accruals and prepayments in the case of wages, materials, rent and insurance:

Example
An examination of the items set out in the trial balance of A Ltd in the previous example reveals the following facts:

1 The wages of £2,300 paid in the first week of February include £700 relating to January.

2 An invoice for £2,000 for material was received in February, although the goods were received in January, and were included in closing stock.

3 The rent paid in January includes £600 referring to the period February to April.

4 The insurance payment of £3,000 has been made in advance and £2,400 relates to the following eleven months, February to December.

From these data, adjust the accounts and set out their effect on the profit and loss statement.

A LTD
EXTRACT FROM PROFIT AND LOSS STATEMENT
For the Month Ended 31 January 19..

	£
Wages	8,700
Materials	27,000
Rent	400
Insurance . . .	600

WAGES ACCOUNT

	£		£
Jan Balance . . .	8,000	Jan Profit & Loss Account .	8,700
Accrual c/d . . .	700		
	8,700		8,700
		Accrual b/d	700

Raw Materials Account

	£		£
Jan Balance b/d . .	25,000	Jan Profit & Loss Account .	27,000
Accrual c/d. . .	2,000		
	27,000		27,000
Feb Invoice . . .	2,000	Accrual b/d . . .	2,000

Rent Account

	£		£
Jan Balance . . .	1,000	Jan Profit & Loss Account .	400
		Prepayment c/d . .	600
	1,000		1,000
Feb Prepayment b/d . .	600		

Insurance Account

	£		£
Jan Balance b/d . .	3,000	Jan Profit & Loss Account .	600
		Prepayment c/d . .	2,400
	3,000		3,000
Feb Prepayment b/d . .	2,400		

It should be noted that the raising of prepayments or accruals adjusts the amount charged to profit and loss account and also that the amount brought down (b/d) will be different, and this difference, as we will see later on in this chapter, will be reflected in the balance sheet.

CLOSING DATA

Closing data will be necessary to finalize the profit and loss statement and balance sheet. These include closing stock, depreciation and provisions for such items as doubtful debts.

Stock

The closing stock is recorded only at the end of each period and at this date opening stock (i.e. the closing stock of the previous period) will be closed off. In fact, the material used during any period is arrived at by taking the opening stock, adding to it the purchase for the period, and deducting the closing stock. The difference will be the material used during the period.

A similar process is carried out by anyone wishing to work out

31

how much he has spent on an evening out on the following morning. First, his opening stock will be the money he had in his pocket the previous morning, the purchase will be what he drew from the bank during yesterday, and his closing stock will be the pitiful collection of coins rattling now in his pockets. By adding the first two items together and subtracting the last, it will be possible to calculate the cost of the previous evening.

To illustrate stock recording, let us examine the following situation and the accounts which are affected.

The closing stock of materials in year 1 of A Ltd amounted to £74,000. During year 2, purchases of material = £780,000. Stock at end of year 2 = £65,000.

STOCK ACCOUNT

	£		£
Year 2 Balance b/f from Year 1	74,000	Year 2 Profit & Loss Account (1) . . .	74,000
Year 2 Profit & Loss Account (3) . . .	65,000		

RAW MATERIAL ACCOUNT

	£		£
Year 2 Sundry Purchases .	780,000	Year 2 Profit & Loss Account (3) . . .	780,000

A LTD

PROFIT AND LOSS ACCOUNT

For Year 2

	£
Opening Stock (1) . .	74,000
Purchases (2) . . .	780,000
	854,000
Less: Closing Stock (3) .	65,000
	789,000

In these entries it should be noted that closing stock is not recorded at all until the profit and loss statement is prepared. The manner of recording the different types of stock such as work in progress and finished goods will be set out and explained in detail when the major illustration shown later in this chapter is discussed.

Depreciation

Depreciation is also an adjustment which is made at the close of any period. It is an accumulated amount and the entry which is required is a charge to the profit and loss statement and an addition to the depreciation built up to the date of the previous final accounts. This is an explanation of the mechanics of recording the item known as depreciation and is illustrated below. A full explanation of what depreciation is and why it is necessary to adjust the final accounts for this item is given at a later stage in this chapter. Here it should be noted that the charge for depreciation must be calculated in order to prepare the final accounts for any period, and management should ensure that these data, i.e. the amount of depreciation, are available for recording well in advance of the final account date.

Illustration

A LTD
EXTRACT FROM TRIAL BALANCE
As at 31 March 19. .

	£	£
Plant and Machinery at cost	90,000	
Depreciation Account		
(Accumulated up to date of previous Profit & Loss Account and Balance Sheet)		30,000

Depreciation of Plant and Machinery for present period computed to be £15,000. Record the necessary entries.

PLANT AND MACHINERY ACCOUNT

	£
Balance b/f* . . .	90,000

DEPRECIATION ACCOUNT (PLANT AND MACHINERY)

	£		£
Balance c/d . . .	45,000	Balance b/f . . .	30,000
		Profit & Loss Account .	15,000
	45,000		45,000
		Balance b/d . . .	45,000

*b/f = Brought forward

33

PROFIT AND LOSS ACCOUNT

For the Period Ended 31 March 19..

£

Depreciation for period   .   15,000

It will be noted that depreciation now stands at £45,000 (£30,000 plus £15,000) and reflects the accumulation of this amount up to the date of the final account.

Provisions

At the close of a period it may be found that there is a need to provide for circumstances which might well lead to an expense or a loss of income, the exact amount of which it may not always be possible to calculate. Such an item might be an amount due to a business from a customer which the evidence of correspondence and other inquiries lead management to believe might never be paid. Such an item is termed a doubtful debt—it is not "bad" yet—and as such it would be wise to adjust for this possible hazard. This is done by making an entry similar to the one illustrated for depreciation, debiting profit and loss account and crediting provision for doubtful debts account. Wherever a situation such as this arises, it is necessary to provide in the final accounts for its possible future effect. It should be noted that provision must be made when the evidence is such as to lead any businessman to believe that a loss of earnings or an expense may arise. There is therefore no choice on the part of management as to whether a provision is or is not to be made. If the evidence points to a possible expense or loss of earnings, a provision *must* be made. Depreciation itself is a provision but in a future illustration we shall be examining the provision for doubtful debts. At this stage we are concerned with a general view of provisions, but the effect and need for provisions will be dealt with later in this chapter. It should be noted that, as with depreciation, management should consider the need for provisions at the date of final account preparation, and this task should be done promptly so that delay is not caused because decisions have not been reached.

Management Choice Adjustments

The adjustments which depend directly upon management decisions concern the distribution of profits and the way in which profits will be shown—an operation sometimes referred to as window-dressing. In both these fields the choice lies with top management, that is, in the case of a limited company, the directors. These adjustments will be illustrated when the extended example is discussed later in this chapter, and it will be seen that they affect the last part of the profit and loss statement, sometimes referred to as the appropriation section.

Summary
Adjustments are the final stage in the production cycle necessary to produce final accounts. If such items are not readily available at the close of any period, the profit and loss statement and balance sheet will be correspondingly delayed. It is, therefore, vital for those concerned with preparing the information to anticipate as far as possible the adjustments which will be required. Certainly in the case of accruals and prepayments much can be done to anticipate these so that at the close of a period the necessary data will be available. This will also be true of provisions and management's policy towards the distribution and retention of profit. In fact, all adjustments can be anticipated to some extent and therefore prepared for either in advance of the final account date, or at least very soon afterwards. The only exception to this rule will be stock if its calculation depends upon a physical count and calculation. Even where this is avoided by means of techniques such as perpetual inventory combined with continual stock records, considerable checking will be required at the final account date, and this will have a delaying effect upon the presentation of the final accounts.

It is, however, suggested that, if all other production steps have been completed as soon as possible after the account date, the clerical staff will be freed to concentrate upon the routines necessary for stock calculation and verification.

Managers' Responsibility in Account Preparation

The need for speed combined with accuracy in the preparation of the profit and loss statement and balance sheet makes it incumbent upon managers to ease bottlenecks and determine whether the reasons given by the presenter of information are satisfactory. For this reason, all managers must be aware of the production processes in the preparation of final accounts and see that steps are taken to ensure speedy and accurate presentation.

To accomplish this objective, the following suggestions are made:

1 Ensure that recording is kept up to date so as to avoid a large volume of recording to be done at the period end.
2 Agreement of the trial balance should take place at least monthly. This will avoid the delays occasioned when differences have to be traced over long periods of time.

3 Adjustments should be anticipated wherever possible so that this does not delay account preparation.

FINAL ACCOUNTS PREPARATION: A FULL TREATMENT

So far, we have been discussing the mechanics of recording and the stages leading up to the presentation of final accounts. It is now necessary to see how these separate mechanics and stages fit into the overall picture of preparing a profit and loss statement and balance sheet.

We shall examine the preparation of the final accounts of a medium-sized limited company and note item by item how each step leads logically to the next. It should be noted that throughout this illustration, in the best tradition of political opposition parties, taxation has been abolished. This is in order to concentrate upon all other aspects of recording and statement presentation. It is considered that taxation requires separate explanation and it is felt that inclusion of this aspect of final accounts would make digestion of the other points more difficult at this stage.

The Illustration: Preparatory Information

Having set the scene, let us now examine the information available within the illustration set out at the end of this chapter. First we have a trial balance and second a list of adjustments. The trial balance shows that A Ltd is a medium-sized manufacturing company with three types of stock, namely finished goods, work in progress and raw materials, and sales, amounting to £1,042,000 for the twelve-month period which is to be presented.

The adjustments show a selection of accruals and prepayments, closing stocks, depreciation, a provision for doubtful debts and certain management choice adjustments regarding profit distribution and transfers to reserve.

This then is the raw material from which to construct the profit and loss statement and balance sheet. It is at this stage, if we look ahead at the final accounts of A Ltd, that we meet a difference. Instead of seeing a profit and loss statement, we find a statement headed "Manufacturing, Trading and Profit and Loss Account," and it is hoped that this will not have the same numbing effect on the reader which the chapter entitled "Magnetism and Electricity" had on me when I had raced through the free and easy opening chapters in my first physics textbook. In fact, we are still dealing with a profit and loss statement, but it has been adapted to the needs of management and divided into three parts.

MANUFACTURING SECTION

The first part deals with the cost of manufacture and is prepared so that management can examine the cost of manufacturing the finished products and compare this with the cost of such products if purchased from an outside source. This has particular importance in certain manufacturing industries such as textiles and speculative building, which have the alternative of self-production or outside purchase, but it is a useful comparison for all manufacturers to make so as to assess their own production efficiency against that of their competitors. Apart from such comparison, it provides management with information to examine the trend over past and present years of manufacturing expenses as a percentage of total manufacturing costs.

TRADING SECTION

The second part, which is called the "Trading Account", calculates the difference between the manufactured cost of goods sold, plus their warehousing expenses and the value of sales. This difference is termed the "gross profit." In a non-manufacturing business such as a wholesale or retail distributor of goods, the gross profit is computed from the difference between the material cost of goods sold and their sales value.

GROSS PROFIT

This profit measure is found to be of real value to managers in assessing the progress of their businesses, first in comparison with past results, and second, and even more importantly, with the result of other enterprises in the same field. This latter advantage owes its popularity to the fact that gross profit has not been subjected, as net profit is, to the deduction of expenses and the inclusion of income which may be relevant only to the particular business under review, and therefore not common to all businesses in the same field. Examples of expenses of this kind would be salaries paid to directors, which may vary from business to business because of the personal circumstances of the people concerned, or rent which will not be payable if property is held freehold. These differences do not relate to the efficiency of carrying on the business and should be ignored when comparing profitability to turnover or sales of similar enterprises.

In the same way, income from investments which are made because surplus funds are available does not relate as such to the particular trade or business under consideration and should be similarly excluded from comparison. Because gross profit is determined before such expenses and incomes have been included, it has particular importance to managers wishing to review the results and profitability of the enterprise and to compare these with those of other similar undertakings.

PROFIT AND LOSS SECTION

The third stage is the profit and loss section, which includes the gross profit as income, plus any non-trading income such as investment interest and provision adjustment. The expenses charged are those concerned with general administration, selling, distribution, finance such as bank charges and interest paid, and any odd or exceptional items. This last category might include such items as a loss on the sale of a fixed asset, or the legal expenses incurred in defending the integrity of an officer of the company.

SUMMARY

It should be noted that this division of what is termed the "revenue statement", in no way affects the final net profit or loss of the enterprise, and is constructed in the manner set out in the example for the benefit of management. There is no legal need to divide the data into three sections and it is therefore the duty of all managers thoroughly to understand and utilize this presentation so that the cost of its production will be justified.

PROFIT AND LOSS STATEMENT

Despite the foregoing explanation of the three divisions, we shall continue to refer to them collectively as the profit and loss statement. However, it is now necessary to examine how each entry has been arrived at in each section, from the trial balance alone, or with the addition or subtraction of the necessary adjustments.

To help the reader follow the entries in the manufacturing, trading and profit and loss sections, a reference is given against each item. Thus, in the case of purchases, which refers to raw materials, the reference is T2 + A1. This means trial balance item 2, purchases, plus the accrual in adjustment 1. This item follows precisely the earlier illustration on page 32. Again, under factory expenses, after the item factory rates is the reference T8 − A11. This refers to trial balance item 8 minus the prepayment in the adjustment 11.

By working carefully through these references and referring back to the previous detailed illustrations in this chapter on adjustments, the reader will be able to follow the construction of each item in the revenue statement. There are, however, certain entries which require further clarification, and these are dealt with below.

Stocks

In the illustration, three different kinds of stocks are shown. These are raw materials and work in progress, dealt with in the manufacturing section, and finished goods, set out in the trading section. The manner in which raw material stock is presented follows exactly the example on stock shown earlier. In this illustration opening stock is added to purchases and closing stock is deducted. On the other hand, both work in progress and finished goods stocks are inset, opening minus closing value, and the difference deducted or added depending upon whether the opening exceeds the closing amount or not. The reader should note that this is simply a change in presentation method and does not alter the fundamental principle of how stock is treated in the final accounts.

In fact, this method of presentation is arrived at to cater specifically for a management need. This need is that changes in stock values between periods are of special interest as they indicate a fluctuation in working capital investment. For this reason it is important for those concerned with investment management to see whether changes have occurred between account dates, and by presenting work in progress and finished goods stock in the manner illustrated, this is clearly shown. The alternative way of presenting these two stocks would be to place the opening stocks at the beginning of the relevant statements and to deduct the closing value at the end. Such separation would make the task of reviewing the difference between the opening and closing amounts somewhat cumbersome. This problem does not apply to raw material stocks which are separated by only one item, namely material purchases, and so comparison between the opening and closing values is eased.

The problem of stock valuation of work-in-progress and finished goods depends on the cost incurred and this is dealt with in Chapter 3. It is, however, worth noting that the general rule of cost or market value whichever is the lower, is the basis used in most industries for raw material stock valuation, whilst in the case of work in progress and finished goods, account must be taken of the labour and overhead expenses which have occurred during manufacture.

The proportion of these expenses to be added will depend upon the progress of manufacture in the stock and will be based upon costing data available within the business.

Discounts Paid and Received

Discounts are the encouragement given to customers or received from suppliers of goods or services for paying within specified periods of time. Thus, in the case of a debtor (someone who owes the business money for goods purchased) a discount may be given if he pays within thirty days or whatever other period is set. The same allowance may be made to a business by its suppliers who, if unpaid, are known as creditors, and they may allow a discount if payment is made to them in accordance with their agreed term. An illustration of these two allowances is set out below:

A Ltd sells goods to B Ltd for £250 and agrees to a discount of two per cent if payment is received within thirty days. The terms are complied with.

A Ltd buys goods from C Ltd for £500 and the terms are three per cent discount if payment is made within one month. A Ltd fulfils these terms. Record these two financial transactions:

B LTD

	£		£
Sales	250	Cash	245
		Discounts paid . . .	5

C LTD

	£		£
Cash	485	Goods	500
Discount received . .	15		

DISCOUNTS PAID

	£		£
B Ltd	5	Profit & Loss Account .	5

DISCOUNTS RECEIVED

	£		£
Profit & Loss Account .	15	C Ltd	15

Debtors and Creditors

The items (T56 and T49) in the trial balance termed "Debtors," "Creditors" are the collective name given, in the case of debtors, to customers who have bought goods on credit and, in the case of creditors, to suppliers from whom the business has bought goods or services on credit. Therefore, debtors represent a number of individual customers whose accounts due to the company amount to £97,358 and creditors represent a number of individual amounts which are due from the company and add up to £67,900.

Interest Received and Paid

Interest is received on investments amounting to £750, item T32 in the trial balance, and this is shown as an item of income in the profit and loss section. Interest paid is the interest due on the debentures, item T48 in the trial balance, and, as such, is a charge against income before arriving at profits.

Unlike dividends, no management choice enters into the decision as to whether or not payment of interest will be made. The question of management choice is dealt with below under the section entitled "Profit Appropriation".

Net Profit or Loss

To understand the nature of net profit or loss it is necessary to stand back from the details of the revenue statement and examine what profit or loss really represents. For this purpose it may be a help to refer back to the key diagram which we discussed in the first chapter and which is repeated as Fig. 4 on page 42.

If we examine the outside circles in the working capital investment (surrounded by the broken line) we will see that the profit and loss statement summarizes the expense of material, labour and overheads and these items are deducted from the income from sales. The expenses and income in the profit and loss statement have been based on the period under review and so stocks have been carried forward and accruals, prepayments and provisions have been adjusted for the period and in accordance with the sales. Nevertheless, the principle of deducting expenses from income is still maintained. It should also be clear that, whereas a profit represents excess income over expense, a loss denotes the opposite situation.

From the key diagram it can be seen that, if sales income exceeds the material, labour and overhead expenses, more cash will flow out of the working capital circle than flowed in, and if the expenses exceed the income, then there will be less. This addition or reduction of cash will then require an adjustment to the investment within the enterprise.

By this reasoning, it can be seen that a profit adds to and a loss reduces the cash, and therefore the capital, in the business. This

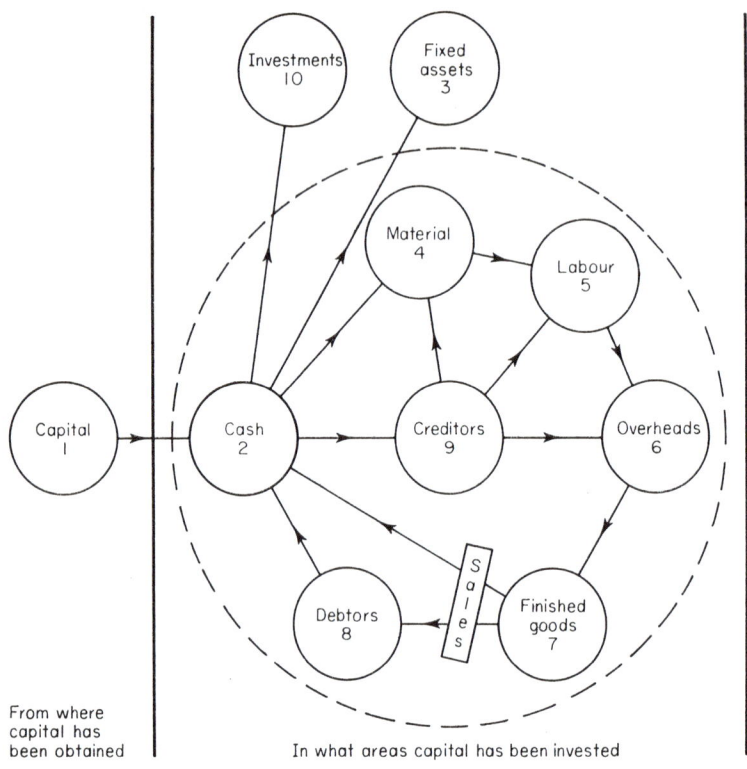

From where
capital has
been obtained

In what areas capital has been invested

FIGURE 4

understanding that profit is an addition to and a loss a reduction of
capital is fundamental to any understanding of financial information
presented for a business.

The Use of Profit or Loss

Whether or not, if a profit is made, such increase will remain in the
enterprise will depend upon the policy of its top management, but
certainly once profit has been earned, it becomes a method of
obtaining additional capital, and in many businesses this is a major
source of this commodity. A net loss means a reduction of capital
within the enterprise.

The ways in which profits of a limited company may be used once
they have been earned are

(i) to increase fixed asset investment; and/or

(ii) to increase working capital investment; and/or
(iii) to increase investment outside the business; and/or
(iv) to distribute to the owners as dividends.

A loss is a reduction of capital invested in the enterprise and as such may be used as follows:

(i) to reduce the fixed asset investment; and/or
(ii) to reduce the outside investment; and/or
(iii) to reduce the working capital invested.

These summaries of what can be done with profits and losses should be clearly understood by all managers who wish to control business investment.

The term "profit planning" is not simply the assessment of what profits will be made by a business, it also concerns itself with where the capital represented by such profits will be invested. The need to plan the use of such profits is paramount as profits are net and therefore the additional capital they represent does not occur at the year or period end, it occurs hourly and daily so long as profits are being made. Planning is equally necessary in the case of losses. In such a case the particular investment or investments which will be reduced should be carefully selected as the wrong choice can worsen what may already be a serious situation.

Depreciation

The way of obtaining additional capital by means of retaining profits within an enterprise is fundamental to understanding depreciation and all other provisions for future losses.

The problem of depreciation can be illustrated from the key diagram (Fig. 5, page 44).

Let us assume that A Ltd starts with an original capital of £420,000 of which £300,000 is invested in fixed assets and £120,000 in working capital. After one year's trading A Ltd makes £60,000 net profit, ignoring taxation, and its directors, being generous, decide to pay out the whole of this profit as a dividend. This is perfectly in order so long as all possible losses have been taken into consideration. But let us suppose that no charge has been made against profits to account for the fact that fixed assets purchased for £300,000 will no longer be worth this amount owing to wear and tear and obsolescence and that their value after taking these factors into account will be only £280,000. In this situation, the capital originally invested in the business has been reduced from £420,000 to £400,000 (fixed assets £280,000 plus working capital £120,000).

43

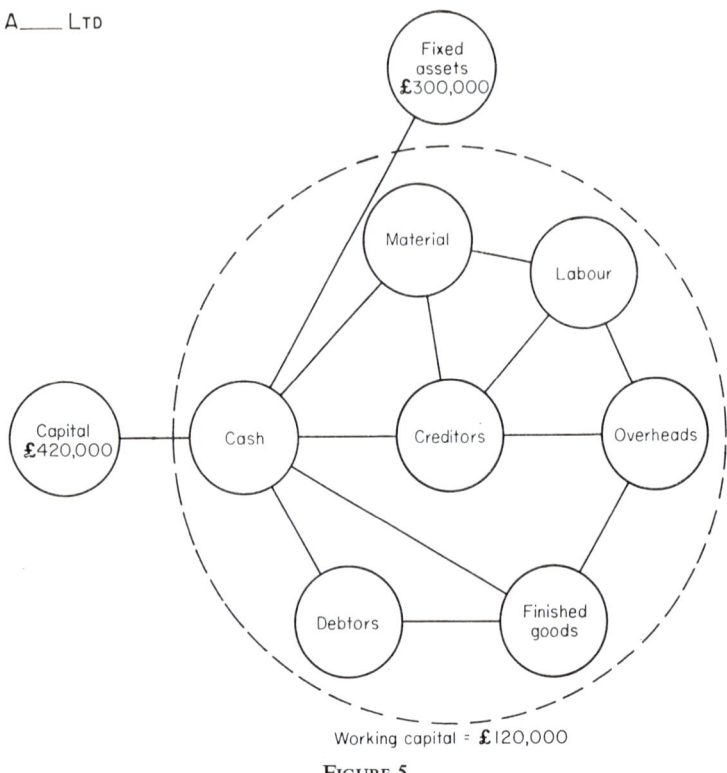

A___ LTD

Working capital = £120,000

FIGURE 5

This situation is not allowed by the law controlling limited companies, which demands that any reduction in value of fixed assets must be replaced out of profits. Depreciation is the method of arranging for this capital replacement and is effected by compulsorily retaining profits. To illustrate this, consider items in the manufacturing section and items in the profit and loss section in the main illustration. Here it will be seen that depreciation (amortization is the word used in the case of leasehold property) is charged as an expense in each of these statements and its effect is to reduce the final net profit shown. However, unlike materials, wages, salaries, rent, insurance, etc., no cash has been spent on depreciation. It is what could be termed a paper deduction, and is simply a word to describe a profit reduction, or in a loss situation, a loss increase. The money therefore represented by this deduction, unlike that for wages, salaries, rents, etc., has not gone out of the business and is still available within the enterprise.

In the major illustration, in addition to the net profit of £97,570, should be added the depreciation items of £16,000 (M10), £3,010 (P7) and £5,000 (P15) to determine the additional cash available for management decision as to reinvestment or distribution during the period under review. However, in the case of depreciation, the management cannot use the cash it represents to distribute as dividends as in the case of net profits.

DEPRECIATION AND ASSET REPLACEMENT

The effect of charging depreciation is therefore to freeze that amount of net profit within the enterprise and create a compulsory retention of this amount. It should be especially noted that charging depreciation in the revenue account does not ensure that when the fixed asset wears out there will be liquid funds available for replacement. If liquid funds will be required, as in the case of a high-cost fixed asset, there must be a corresponding investment in a cashable security or insurance policy.

This must be fully understood by management so that they are not lulled into a false sense of well-being simply because they have made the necessary depreciation deduction from profit. If they are likely to require the liquid funds when replacement takes place, they must arrange their investment policy accordingly.

DEPRECIATION: DETERMINING THE AMOUNT

The depreciation required for each fixed asset should be calculated by those who are familiar with the use and provision of each item and this may not be anyone connected with the financial function, but could be, for instance, the plant manager or the sales manager. The amount required for each period should be calculated in the light of experience regarding wear and tear and obsolescence and this should be communicated to the presenter of the information. To illustrate depreciation, let us take the following situation:

A Ltd buys a piece of plant and machinery for £50,000. The plant manager calculates that its life will be five years and he estimates its scrap value at the end of its life to be £10,000. Compile the annual depreciation charge:

		£
Cost of Fixed Asset .	.	50,000
Less scrap value .	.	10,000
Balance to Depreciate	.	40,000

Annual depreciation $\frac{1}{5} \times$ £40,000 = £8,000.
This is termed the straight-line method of depreciation.

An alternative method is known as the reducing balance method and this requires a percentage rate to be calculated which is used to reduce the balance remaining each year. To illustrate this method, taking the facts set out in the previous example, let us assume a rate of 30 per cent depreciation and ignore scrap value:

				£
	Cost of Fixed Asset.			50,000
Year 1 *Less* Depreciation			.	16,667
				33,333
Year 2	,,	,,	.	11,111
				22,222
Year 3	,,	,,	.	7,407
				14,815
Year 4	,,	,,	.	4,938
				9,877
Year 5	,,	,,	.	3,292
				6,585

DEPRECIATION: GENERAL

It should be noted that depreciation is based on the cost of the fixed asset and not the replacement value, however different this may appear to be. Thus, at the end of the life of a fixed asset, depreciation will have been charged only up to its original cost less any scrap value. This may be far less than the cost of replacement and it has been suggested that for this reason the depreciation charge is unrealistic. The answer to this criticism is that depreciation is based on what is definitely known, and this is the cost of fixed assets. The belief that replacement cost will be in excess of this amount is deduction, and as such cannot be classed as depreciation. However, this does not mean that steps cannot be taken to provide for this anticipated additional amount, but it will not be adjusted in the depreciation charge. Such sums will be raised through named reserves which will be dealt with under the head "Profit Appropriation".

Provisions

It will be seen from the examination of depreciation that a deduction from profit by a charge which is not represented by a cash payment out of the business is a method of compulsory capital retention. In the case of depreciation, this capital retention replaces the corresponding loss in the value of fixed assets and therefore the total capital invested is kept constant, but this method of retention may be used for other purposes. For instance, where it is anticipated that certain customers who owe money for sales (i.e. debtors) will not pay, but no definite proof of this is obtainable, it would be right to retain profit up to this amount and therefore have available within the business additional capital to compensate for such possible future loss.

This anticipation of possible future losses of investment, which might take place under the separate heads of fixed assets, investment or working capital, must be compensated by the raising of the appropriate provision. It should be noted that, in the case of working capital, because of its net nature (current assets less current liabilities), loss of investment may take the form of a loss of stock or debtors, or an increase in a creditor.

DOUBTFUL DEBT PROVISION

We shall now take one particular provision and examine it in detail, namely the provision for doubtful debts. In this particular case we shall first examine the specific example and then we shall apply the principle to the major illustration.

Example

X Ltd sold goods to the customers listed below for the following amounts:

	£
A.B. & Co.	100
S.J. Ltd.	50
D.Q. & Co.	1,200
L.S. Ltd	410

During the next few months the following circumstances arose: A.B. & Co. became bankrupt and the statement of affairs showed it unlikely that X Ltd would receive more than 10p in the £. D.Q. & Co. paid. In the case of S.J. Ltd and L.S. Ltd, after invoices and statements had been rendered, and much correspondence conducted and many telephone calls made, the amounts due were still unpaid and it was decided to provide for the amounts due. Record this information in the account of X Ltd.

X LTD BOOKS OF ACCOUNT
A.B. & Co.

				£					£
Balance b/f	.	.	.	100	(1) Bad Debts	.	.	.	90
					Balance c/d	.	.	.	10
				100					100
Balance c/d	.	.	.	10					

S.J. Ltd

		£
Balance b/f . . .		50

D.Q. & Co

		£					
Balance b/f . . .		1,200	Cash				1,200

L.S. Ltd

		£
Balance b/f . . .		400

Bad Debts

		£
(1) A.B. & Co . . .		90

Provision for Doubtful Debt

	£
(2) Profit & Loss Account .	450

Y LTD
Profit and Loss Statement
For the Period Ended 31 March 19. .

		£
(1) Bad Debts . . .		90
(2) Provision for Doubtful Debts . . .		450

It will be noted from this illustration that, by providing for S.J. Ltd and L.S. Ltd, the net profit shown has been reduced by £450. The £450 additional capital is retained within the business to cover any possible future loss which may arise if either of these two customers fail to pay.

On the other hand, the bad debt is written off against profit. It should be especially noted that only bad debts are written off, and even in this case, if it is felt that any amount is likely to be received, the amount is left in the account. The practice of leaving amounts due on the personal accounts of customers is one which ensures action will continue to be taken to collect the debts. It also prevents the danger that might arise if a customer pays at a later date and there is no record of such an amount due. This record omission has been known to lead to theft on the part of the receiving cashier.

48

In the case of the larger illustration we have a situation which may require some clarification. Item 35 in the trial balance shows the provision for doubtful debts to be £1,500. This is the amount which it was felt necessary to provide based on the amount due from customers at the end of the previous year. Since this date the situation will have changed considerably. Some debtors will have paid and others will have become bad debts and, when the debtors are examined at the present year end, the amount due which is believed to be doubtful shown in the adjustment item 19 is £1,200.

The provision of doubtful debts is illustrated below:

PROVISION FOR DOUBTFUL DEBTS

	£		£
Profit & Loss Account .	300	Balance b/f . . .	1,500
Balance c/f . . .	1,200		
	1,500		1,500
		Balance c/f . . .	1,200

The reduction in the provision required in this case enables £300 to be released and this amount is added back to profit (see profit and loss statement item).

Profit Appropriation

The choice of management as to how they will deal with profit is limited to the appropriation section. This section is shown in the main illustration after the net profit of £97,570 has been arrived at. In this part of the revenue account are shown items such as dividends, i.e. the distributions, and the transfer to reserves. On the income side is set out the net profit for the present year and added to this is the balance of profit brought forward from the previous period of £29,110. This is item 40 on the trial balance and is a cumulative balance as at the date of the last final account. It does not indicate the profit or loss for the previous period and corresponds with the balance at the close of this account of £64,680.

TRANSFERS TO RESERVES

Transfers to reserves are sometimes referred to cynically as "window dressing". This is because it has become the habit of some boards of directors to make transfers to rather grand-sounding reserves and by this method reduce the amount shown under the heading "profit and loss balance".

49

This practice is encouraged by the separation which has grown over recent years in some businesses between the interests of investors and managers. This dichotomy of interests is caused by investors seeking higher and higher dividends and directors wishing to retain more and more profits as a source of additional capital to plough back into the enterprise. For this reason it is felt that the less shown under the title "profit and loss balance", the less will the shareholders feel that they have received too niggardly a dividend. As transfers to reserves have the effect of reducing the amount shown under the title "profit and loss balance", such entries have considerable attraction to directors in this situation.

These transfers ensure nothing except that this amount of profit will not be distributed to shareholders. The amount shown, such as the £40,000 transferred to general reserve in the illustration of A Ltd, will be left in the enterprise, but exactly where it will be invested rests upon the decision of management rather than the title of the reserve. Thus a dividend equalization reserve, which is often presented as a reserve available for the payment of dividends in future years should profits be insufficient, does not guarantee that liquid funds (i.e. cash or easily encashed items) will be available to pay dividends in such circumstances. The additional capital will certainly be invested within the business but exactly where it is located will depend upon the investment decisions of the directors.

Transfers to reserves are therefore a way of retaining profits, but the names given to such items are an indication of intention more than a definite commitment of funds within the enterprise for the stated purpose.

A further illustration of this point can be seen in the accounts of A Ltd. The reserve for the excess cost of replacing fixed assets, item 47 on the trial balance, indicates the purpose of holding back more profits than is possible under depreciation to account for the increased replacement cost. However, whether or not the liquid funds will be available when the fixed assets require replacement will depend on the investment policy of the directors of A Ltd, in the same way as explained in the section on depreciation.

DIVIDENDS

The dividends shown in this section for A Ltd are divided between those which have been paid and those which are proposed. The paid dividend is the interim dividend paid during the year to assist shareholders before the final dividend can be declared and paid. This interim dividend is shown in the trial balance as item 39. However, the final dividend of £17,500 and the preference dividend of £1,500 are proposed only when the results of the year are known, and these are not shown in the trial balance but appear under the adjustments item 23.

The amount of the dividend will depend upon the terms of the shares issued and, if on preference shares, will be normally a fixed rate per share. In the case of ordinary shares, often referred to as the equity of the company, the dividend will be determined by the policy of the directors, but this will be greatly influenced by the profitability of the enterprise, and to some extent the pressure of the ordinary shareholders. This pressure, which is strengthened by the fact that ordinary shareholders have voting rights which determine the composition of the board of directors, cannot be altogether ignored!

BALANCE SHEET

The balance sheet to the book-keeper and to far too many accountants is exactly what it says it is, a sheet of balances. However, for any use to be made of it, it must be recognized as a summary of investment within the business and of the sources from which the capital invested has been obtained.

From the point of view of recording mechanics, the balance sheet is in fact a list of the balances that are left after the completion of the profit and loss statement. If we stand back from these data it will be seen that the profit and loss statement has had the effect of closing off many of the balances shown in the trial balance, although in some cases fresh balances have been created as in the case of accruals, prepayments, stocks, provisions and reserves. In the illustration on page 61, as in the case of the profit and loss statement, a reference is placed against each balance sheet item so that the way it has been built up can be followed.

However, our chief concern is understanding the information that a balance sheet contains and such understanding must start from recognizing a clear division between the sources and the application of capital.

Clarity is not facilitated by the way balance sheets are sometimes presented and in the case of A Ltd two layouts of this statement are produced so that the two basic methods of presentation can be compared. Irrespective of which method of presentation is adopted, we shall now examine the contents of the balance sheet.

Sources of Capital

As explained in this and the previous chapter, there are several sources of capital for any business. These are the owners' own capital, long-term loans and retained profits. This latter source is really the owners' capital, as profits, whether distributed or not, all belong to the proprietors.

In the case of limited companies, the sources of capital become share capital (proprietors), debentures, mortgages, loans over five years or more (long-term loans) and reserves (retained profits). We shall now discuss these items as they appear in the illustration of A Ltd.

Share Capital

The first point which must be understood is that the share capital is presented in a particular manner. First, authorized share capital is set out and this is the share capital which the company is authorized to issue by the terms of its incorporation. This authorized share capital is not part of the double-entry recording. It is a form of note and is set out in the balance sheet for the interest of those reading it, so that they can see how much share capital can still be issued without expanding the authorized capital.

The column headed "issued and fully paid" is the part which is recorded in the books of account and the heading refers to the fact that these shares have been issued for the amount due, namely £1, and that the full amount has been paid up on each share. In some circumstances it might be found useful to issue shares and call only part of the amount due, e.g. £1 shares on which 50p is called up. In this situation the remainder due, viz. 50p, can be called up when it is required and in the meantime the column would be divided to show the number of shares issued and then a separate column would be provided for the amount called up. The share capital of A Ltd consists of 6 per cent preference shares and ordinary shares. The 7 per cent preference shares have been issued, but at the date of the balance sheet they have also been fully redeemed.

Reserves

As explained when dealing with the profit and loss statement, the name "reserve" is used to refer to profits retained within the business. In most cases the retention of profits follows the direct decision of the company's directors such as the creation of general reserve, the reserve for the excess cost of replacing fixed assets or again the balance left on the profit and loss account. However, there are two reserves that have to be created following certain situations and these two reserves differ from all the others in that once they are created they can never be used to pay out dividends.

To pay out a dividend two commodities must be present, first, available profits, and second, cash. It may be thought that cash is more important than profit in this connection, but in practice cash may be borrowed or items may be sold to obtain it, whereas the production of profits, if they have not been made by a company, is beyond the immediate capability of any board of directors. It must be noted that the transfer of amounts out of the profit and loss statement to reserve does not prevent their use for future dividend payments as they are still profits available for distribution whatever their names may be.

The two reserves which do not follow this rule and which are dealt with below are the share premiums and the capital redemption reserve fund. Neither of these two reserves—sometimes referred to as "capital reserves"—can be used to distribute dividends.

SHARE PREMIUMS

The share premium is the profit which arises when shares are issued at more than their nominal value. Such an issue is normal once a business has been operating for any length of time and considerable reserves have been built up. In such circumstances, the nominal value of the ordinary shares will in no way represent their real value, as it will be remembered that profits, whether paid out or retained, still belong to the shareholders who have the right to vote.

For this reason, when additional voting-right shares are issued it will be normal to issue them at their commercial rather than their nominal value, and this will involve in most cases issuing at a premium. The premium is the difference between the issue price and the nominal value, and is recorded as a share premium reserve, as the following example will explain:

Example

50,000 £1 Ordinary Shares are issued by S Ltd, at £1·50 each. Record this issue.

ORDINARY SHARE CAPITAL ACCOUNT

	£
Cash	50,000

SHARE PREMIUM ACCOUNT

	£
Cash	25,000

CASH ACCOUNT

			£
Ordinary Share	.	.	50,000
Share Premium	.	.	25,000

CAPITAL REDEMPTION RESERVE FUND

The capital redemption reserve fund is the reserve which must be set up in the case of the redemption of shares when, at the same time, no fresh issue of share capital takes place to compensate for the redemption. This rule, which is contained in the Companies Act, is for the purpose of guaranteeing outsiders dealing with any company as to the amount of the permanent capital invested.

To illustrate this point, let us examine the following situation:

X LTD

BALANCE SHEET (EXTRACT)

As at 31 March 19..

	£
SHARE CAPITAL (Authorized, Issued & Fully Paid) .	
7% Redeemable Preference Shares 100,000	100,000
Ordinary Shares 200,000	200,000
	300,000
RESERVES	
Profit & Loss Balance 200,000	200,000
	500,000

The outsiders' guarantee of permanent capital within X Ltd is £300,000.

If redeemable preference shares are redeemed and no fresh share capital is issued in their place, the following entries must be made: profit and loss balance must be reduced and a capital redemption reserve fund created for the same value.

The revised balance sheet in these circumstances will be as follows:

X LTD

BALANCE SHEET (EXTRACT)

As at 31 March 19..

SHARE CAPITAL	Authorized £	Issued and Fully Paid £	£
7% Red. Pref. Shares	100,000	—	—
Ordinary Shares	200,000	200,000	200,000
	300,000		
RESERVES			
Capital Redemption Reserve Fund .		100,000	
Profit & Loss Account . . .		100,000	
			200,000
			400,000

It will be seen that the capital redemption reserve fund is created out of a reserve which otherwise would be available for distribution in the form of dividends. The transfer has therefore the effect of freezing the amount involved (£100,000 in the example) within the business.

OTHER RESERVES

No further comment is needed on the other reserves as they have been referred to earlier in the text. It will be noted that the general reserve has been increased by £40,000 this year from its former amount, and that the reserve for excess cost of replacing fixed assets is left unchanged at £40,000. The reserve entitled capital reserve £20,000 is also unchanged and its title indicates an intention on the part of the directors never to use this sum for dividend distribution. It should, however, be noted that this is the directors' intention, and is not in any way legally enforceable. In other words, this intention could be reversed by a change in the board of directors brought about by the votes of the ordinary shareholders.

Long-term Loan

In the case of A Ltd, £10,000 has been obtained by a debenture issue at 5 per cent interest. A debenture is a long-term loan evidenced in writing and normally secured on an investment or investments within the business.

The Application of Capital

A Ltd has therefore obtained capital from share capital to the extent of £175,000, from reserves £369,680 and from debenture £10,000 which totals £554,680 and it is now necessary to examine how this amount has been invested. The investment of A Ltd is divided into the three main categories of fixed assets, investments and working capital, and the individual items under each head can be followed with the assistance of the references placed against each item.

The reader is advised to follow carefully the build-up of each item, and the key diagram might be found useful to examine the snapshot nature of the balance sheet.

The sub-heading "current assets and current liabilities", which may confuse the reader, is represented in the outside and inside circles of the working capital investment in the key diagram. The word "current" refers to the fact that the assets are, or will become, cash during the near future and the liabilities are the debts which have to be met during the near future. Thus, working capital of nil means that current assets equal current liabilities.

Conclusion

It is most important that any confusion caused by the jargon of financial accounting should be eliminated. To tell whether this is so it is vital for each entry in the profit and loss statement and balance sheet to be fully understood in the simplest possible terms. It is only when the confusion of terms and expressions has been eliminated that understanding and interpretation of final accounts can begin.

At this stage the reader should be able to understand the mechanics of preparing the final accounts and to follow the necessity for each statement. The problem of interpretation of these data by management is dealt with in Chapter 7 but at present it is necessary to establish a foundation of understanding upon which interpretation can be built.

A LTD

TRIAL BALANCE

as at 31 December 1971

	£	£
(T1) Raw Material Stock 1 Jan. 1971	65,240	
(T2) Purchases	362,000	
(T3) Direct Labour	208,050	
(T4) Factory Manager's Salary	15,200	
(T5) Foremen's Wages	6,000	
(T6) Indirect Factory Wages	55,100	
(T7) Factory Rent	3,050	
(T8) Factory Rates	1,500	
(T9) Factory Insurance	2,030	
(T10) Depreciation Plant & Machinery . . .		182,200
(T11) Work in Progress Stock 1 Jan. 1971 . . .	98,200	
(T12) Warehouse Manager's Salary	2,600	
(T13) Storemen's Wages	5,000	
(T14) Warehouse Rent	450	
(T15) Warehouse Rates	400	
(T16) Finished Goods Stock 1 Jan. 1971 . . .	115,000	
(T17) Admin. Managers Salaries	48,315	

Total Carried Forward £988,135 £182,200

T = Trial balance items
A = Adjustment items
M = Manufacturing section
Tr = Trading section
P = Profit and loss section

	£	£
Totals b/f	£988,135	£182,200
(T18) Office Salaries	31,002	
(T19) Office Rent	1,300	
(T20) Office Rates	640	
(T21) Office Insurance	720	
(T22) Stationery	3,412	
(T23) Office Equipment Depreciation		26,090
(T24) Sales Managers' Salaries	16,000	
(T25) Salesmen's Salaries	40,500	
(T26) Salesmen's Commission	36,000	
(T27) Sales Office Rent & Rates	6,000	
(T28) Bad Debts	4,100	
(T29) Advertising	42,050	
(T30) Printing & Stationery	7,500	
(T31) Amortization of Lease		20,000
(T32) Interest on Investments		750
(T33) Discounts Received		2,100
(T34) Sales		1,042,000
(T35) Doubtful Debt Provision 1 Jan. 1971		1,500
(T36) Discounts Paid	1,020	
(T37) Bank Charges	3,053	
(T38) Interest Paid	500	
(T39) Dividend Paid	3,000	
(T40) Net Profit Carried Forward		29,110
(T41) 6% Preference Shares		25,000
(T42) Ordinary Shares		150,000
(T43) Share Premium Account		25,000
(T44) Capital Redemption Reserve Fund		100,000
(T45) Capital Reserve		20,000
(T46) General Reserve		80,000
(T47) Reserve for Excess Cost of Replacing Fixed Assets		40,000
(T48) 5% Debentures		10,000
(T49) Creditors		67,900
(T50) Bank Overdraft		42,010
(T51) Freehold Land & Buildings—Cost	145,210	
(T52) Leasehold Property—Cost	50,000	
(T53) Plant & Machinery—Cost	330,000	
(T54) Office Equipment—Cost	46,050	
(T55) Investment—7,500 £1 Shares in X Ltd	6,010	
(T56) Debtors	97,358	
(T57) Bank	4,100	
	£1,863,660	£1,863,660

57

5

NOTES   £

Accruals as at 31 Dec. 1971

		£
(A1)	Raw Material	3,000
(A2)	Direct Labour	2,000
(A3)	Foremen's Wages	300
(A4)	Factory Indirect Wages	3,300
(A5)	Warehouse Wages	400
(A6)	Office Salaries	1,100
(A7)	Office Rent	200
(A8)	Salesmen's Salaries	1,500
(A9)	Salesmen's Commission	2,000
(A10)	Sales Rent & Rates	20

                                                          (A24)   £13,820

Prepayments as at 31 Dec. 1971

		£
(A11)	Factory Rates	400
(A12)	Warehouse Rates	150
(A13)	Office Rates	120
(A14)	Office Insurance	72

                                                           (A25)   £742

		£
(A15)	Transfer to General Reserve for Year	£40,000

Stocks as at 31 Dec. 1971

		£
(A16)	Raw Material	73,040
(A17)	Work in Progress	106,400
(A18)	Finished Goods	92,000

                                                            £271,440

		£
(A19)	Provision for Doubtful Debts 31 Dec. 1971 to be . .	£1,200

Depreciation to be charged for year ended 31 Dec. 1971

		£
(A20)	Plant and Machinery	16,000
(A21)	Office Equipment	3,010
(A22)	Amortization of Lease	5,000

                                                            £24,010

		£
(A23)	Proposed Dividend for the Year.	£19,000

A LTD
Manufacturing, Trading and Profit and Loss Account
For the Year Ended 31 December 1971

				£	£	£
	Raw Materials					
(M1)	Stock 1 January 1971	(T1) .	. .	65,240	Cost of	
(M2)	Purchases	(T2 + A1) .	. . .	365,000	Manufactured	
					Goods c/f 661,130	
(M3)				430,240		
	Less Stock 31 December 1971 (A16)		. .	73,040		
					357,200	
	Direct Labour (T3 + A2) .		. .		210,050	
	Prime Cost				567,250	
	Factory Expenses					
(M4)	Manager's Salary (T4) .		. .	15,200		
(M5)	Foremen's Wages (T5 + A3)		. .	6,300		
(M6)	Indrect Factory Wages (T6 + A4)		. .	58,400		
(M7)	Factory Rent (T7) .		. .	3,050		
(M8)	Factory Rates (T8 — A11) .	.	. .	1,100		
(M9)	Factory Insurance (T9) .	.	. .	2,030		
(M10)	Depreciation on Plant & Machinery (A20)			16,000		
					102,080	
					669,330	
	Less W.I.P. Stock					
(M11)	As at 1 January 1971 (T11)		. .	98,200		
(M12)	*Less* as at 31 December 1971 (A17)		.	106,400		
					8,200	
					£661,130	£661,130

Manufacturing
Section

59

Trading Section

		£		£
Cost of Manufactured Goods b/f . .		661,130	SALES	1,042,000
WAREHOUSE EXPENSES	£			
(Tr1) Manager's Salary (T12)	2,600			
(Tr2) Storemen's Wages (T13 + A5)	5,400			
(Tr3) Warehouse Rent (T14)	450			
(Tr4) Warehouse Rates (T15 − A12) . .	250	8,700		
		669,830		
Add: Finished Goods Stock				
(Tr5) As at 1 January 1971 .	115,000 (T16)			
(Tr6) *Less:* as at 31 Dec. 1971 (A18) . .	92,000	23,000		
		692,830		
GROSS PROFIT c/d .		349,170		
		£1,042,000		£1,042,000

Profit and Loss Section

	£		£
(P1) Managers' Salaries (T17) . .	48,315	Gross Profit b/d	349,170
(P2) Salaries (T18 + A6) . .	32,102	(P22) Interest on	
(P3) Office Rent (T19 + A7) .	1,500	Investments (T32)	750
(P4) Office Rates (T20 − A13) .	520	(P23) Doubtful Debts	
(P5) Insurance (T21 − A14) .	648	Recovered (T35 − A19)	300
(P6) Stationery (T22) . . .	3,412	(P24) Discounts	
(P7) Office Equipment Depreciation (A21)	3,010	Received (T33)	2,100
(P8) Sales Managers' Salaries (T24) .	16,000		
(P9) Salesmen's Salaries (T25 + A8) .	42,000		
(P10) Salesmen's Commission (T26 + A9)	38,000		
(P11) Sales Office Rent & Rates (T27 + A10)	6,020		
(P12) Bad Debts (T28) . . .	4,100		
(P13) Advertising (T29) .	42,050		
(P14) Printing & Stationery (T30) .	7,500		
(P15) Amortization of Lease (A22) .	5,000		
(P16) Discounts Paid (T36) . .	1,020		
(P17) Bank Charges (T37) . .	3,053		
(P18) Interest Paid (T38) . .	500		
Net Profit c/d	97,570		
	352,320		352,320
Transfers to:		Net Profit b/d	97,570
(P19) General Reserve (A15) .	40,000	(P25) Net Profit b/f (T40)	29,110
(P20) Interim Dividend Paid (T39) .	3,000		
(P21) Final Dividend Proposed (A23)	19,000		
(P26) Balance c/f	64,680		
	£126,680		£126,680

A LTD
BALANCE SHEET
As at 31 December 1971

SHARE CAPITAL	Authorized £	Issued & Fully Paid £	£	£
7% Redeemable Preference Shares	100,000	— (T41)		
6% Preference Shares	50,000	25,000 (T42)		
Ordinary Shares	200,000	150,000		175,000
RESERVES				
Share Premium Account		25,000 (T43)		
Capital Redemption Reserve Fund		100,000 (T44)		
Capital Reserve		20,000 (T45)	145,000	
General Reserve		120,000 (T46 + P19)		
Reserve for Excess Cost of replacing Fixed Asset		40,000 (T47)		
Profit & Loss Account		64,680 (P27)	224,680	369,680
				544,680
5% Debentures				10,000 (T48)
				554,680
CURRENT LIABILITIES				
Creditors		67,900 (T49)		
Accruals		13,820 (A24)		
Bank Overdraft		42,010 (T50)		
Proposed Dividends		19,000 (P21)		142,730
				£697,410

FIXED ASSETS	Cost £	Depreciation to Date £	£	£
Freehold Land & Buildings (T51)	145,210	—		145,210
Leasehold Property (T53)	50,000	25,000 (T31 + P15)		25,000
Plant & Machinery (T53)	330,000	198,200 (T10 + M10)		131,800
Office Equipment (T54)	46,050	29,100 (T23 + P7)		16,950
	571,260	252,300		318,960
INVESTMENTS				
7,500 £1 shares in X Ltd (T55)				6,010
CURRENT ASSETS				
Raw Material Stock (M3)		73,040		
Work in Progress Stock (M12)		106,400		
Finished Goods Stock (Tr6)		92,000		
Debtors & Prepayments (T56 + A25)	98,100			
Less Provisions for Doubtful Debts (A19)	1,200	96,900		
Bank (T57)		4,100		
				372,440
				£697,410

A LTD

BALANCE SHEET

as at 31 December 1971

(Alternative Presentation)

FIXED ASSETS	Cost	Depreciation to Date		
	£	£	£	£
Freehold Land & Buildings . .	145,210	—		145,210
Leasehold Property . . .	50,000	25,000		25,000
Plant & Machinery . . .	330,000	198,200		131,800
Office Equipment	46,050	29,100		16,950
	571,260	252,300		318,960

INVESTMENTS				
7,500 £1 shares in X Ltd . . .				6,010

CURRENT ASSETS				
Raw Material Stock . . .		73,040		
Work in Progress Stock . . .		106,400		
Finished Goods Stock . . .		92,000		
Debtors & Prepayments . . .	98,100			
Less Provision for Doubtful Debts .	1,200			
. . . . . .		96,900		
Bank		4,100		
			372,440	

CURRENT LIABILITIES				
Creditors		67,900		
Accruals		13,820		
Bank Overdraft		42,010		
Proposed Dividends . . .		19,000		
			142,730	229,710
				554,680

A LTD

Financed by:

SHARE CAPITAL

	Authorized	Issued and Fully Paid		
	£	£	£	£
7% Redeemable Preference Shares .	100,000	—		
6% Preference Shares . . .	50,000	25,000		
Ordinary Shares	200,000	150,000		
				175,000

RESERVES

Share Premium Account . . .		25,000		
Capital Redemption Reserve Fund .		100,000		
Capital Reserve		20,000		
			145,000	
General Reserve		120,000		
Reserve for Excess Cost of replacing				
Fixed Assets		40,000		
Profit & Loss Account . . .		64,680		
			224,680	
				369,680
				544,680
5% Debentures				10,000
				554,680

63

3   *Costing*

In the beginning there was an inquiring manager presented with a profit and loss statement and in the end there was a costing system. Costing is a clear example of how the thoughtful manager has influenced the development of financial information. The profit and loss statement sets out the net profit or net loss for the stated period but if more than one product or service is produced, no indication is given as to exactly where such profit or loss has arisen.

THE APPROACH TO ANALYSIS

The answer to this problem is to analyse the expenses and income in whichever way is suitable to the needs of the enterprise. Once such analysis has been set in motion it often creates in itself a demand for further analysis. More and more breakdown is found necessary and a basic costing system which involves the analysis of expense and income under products or services is found to be inadequate for management purposes. Supplementary analysis develops and the increase in analysis may take the form of costing to stages of production. For example, the cost of production in the conversion mill or the machine shop or the cost of rendering part of the service.

Again, such analysis may be extended to areas of management supervision or geographical location within the business, known as cost centres. These cost centres are eventually allocated to the main cost unit and will be explained later in this chapter. Examples of a cost centre might be a section within the general administration department or a batch of machines within the factory or the welfare function of a departmental store.

MANAGEMENT AND THE PROBLEMS OF ANALYSIS

This extension of analysis presents management with two problems: first, the control of expenses in these smaller areas, and second, the increase which will occur in the cost of a costing system. The manager must be aware of his responsibility under both these heads, the first of which is dealt with under the title "The Analysis of Expenses" later in this chapter. As regards the second problem, the cost of a costing system must be closely supervised by management to see that an adequate return is obtained on the expenditure involved. This problem is one which it is difficult for management to assess with any degree of accuracy. However, it is important for all those who receive costing information to be quite sure that it is of real use to themselves and to the enterprise as a whole.

This need to stand back from costing data and ask oneself the simple question "What are their use?" is often lacking in modern business, yet it is suggested that this questioning approach is vital unless the cost of such data presentation is to get right out of hand. Costing is a detailed technique. It is a system of analysis which over the years of its development has sometimes become lost in its own jargon and therefore meaningless. For this reason every costing system needs the cool questioning approach of the manager who has not been involved in the collection and presentation of the data.

Once again the temptation to delegate understanding must be resisted and all managers must recognize that the data presented stem from the specific requests of present and past managers. For this reason care should be taken to see that their needs are still being catered for and that the data are relevant.

CHOOSING THE COST UNIT

Costing is analysis of expenses and income to a cost unit and the first step in setting up a costing system is to select the unit for the particular business. Such a unit is normally chosen to fit the output of the business. Thus, in an industry concerned with manufacture, the unit selected will be the manufactured item and in a service industry the unit will be the service rendered. This rule, however, is adapted in each enterprise to suit the specific demands of management and the circumstances of production or service rendering.

COSTING SYSTEMS

Thus, in the case of batch production, expenses and income are related to the particular batch and the cost per product is found by dividing the total cost by the number of products in each batch. The cost of one unit is therefore an average cost. Again, in the case of the chemical, paint or oil industry, where production passes through processes or stages, the costing system is arranged to determine the cost of each process and the unit which might be so many litres or kilograms will be an average cost of the process.

Where production has no natural beginning or end, the costing analysis is arranged around a period of time, say, a month, week or day. Examples of such production would be coal-mining and flow-line motor-car production. In this situation the cost of production during these periods of time is divided by the selected unit of output and, as in the case of batch and process production, an average cost calculated. Conversely, in industries concerned with the production of one item such as a ship, a bridge or a piece of costume jewellery, the costs will be identified to the specific unit produced.

A service will be costed in a similar manner to a manufactured product but the presentation will be related to the management needs of the industry. In this area reference is made to the cost per hospital bed, or the cost per ton or passenger mile in transport, and the costs will again be based on an average calculation, whereas the cost of rendering a service such as management consultancy will be analysed to the specific assignment and an average cost will not apply.

Much work is still necessary in many service industries to relate costing systems to the specific needs of their management and this fact will be taken into account when we deal with the computation and control of expenses.

It should be especially noted that the cost unit is selected to suit the particular business to which it is applied. The major division between methods of costing is whether it is possible to arrive at a specific cost, termed a "job cost", or whether it is only possible to compute an average cost. When the latter situation exists the method of costing is termed "process costing".

It should be recognized by managers that it is their responsibility to make sure the cost unit is suitable to their need to control the expense and income of the enterprise under their control.

THE ANALYSIS OF EXPENSES

Whichever cost unit is selected, it will be necessary to analyse expenses to it. This will involve the setting up of controls for each item of expense to make sure that all expenses are charged to one product or service or another and also that the correct charge has been made against the right item. This dual aspect of analysis control must be understood as its effectiveness or otherwise lies at the root of all costing systems.

CONTROL OF EXPENSES

The cynic's comment that more businesses have failed because they had a costing system rather than because they had not, owes its truth, if any, to one or other of these controls being missing. Too often it is found that, although expenses are charged to the right product or service, a large volume of expense is never taken into consideration in the analysis at all.

If control in reconciling the individual costs with the total expenses is lacking or if accurate analysis does not take place, the costs will be inaccurate and the manager taking action based on such false data may easily be committing the enterprise to most dangerous policies. Such action could be to decide to concentrate sales on a particular product or service based on the costs which show a particular rate of profit. If this proves inaccurate it could have a disastrous effect upon the future profitability of the business. The foundation of every costing system must therefore be the establishment of expense controls and, in the case of material and labour, these will take the form of what are termed "physical controls". Such physical controls imply that every unit of material and labour is correctly charged to one unit of production or another and that the total material and labour usage of the business is fully accounted for.

COST PRESENTATION

To illustrate the underlying need to control expenses, we shall now examine the presentation of the costs of three products for a manufacturing business. In this illustration, it should be noted how expenses are divided into elements such as direct material, direct labour, works expenses, etc., and that these elements are subtotalled into the stage costs known as prime cost, works cost, cost of production and cost of sales.

It should also be understood that the costs presented for a service or other non-manufacturing industry will differ only in that there will in most cases be fewer divisions or elements of expense. There will, however, still be expenses which are direct as opposed to indirect and the principles will remain unchanged.

The necessity for two-way control of expenses is to ensure, as explained above, first that the right material, labour and other

67

A LTD

	Products		
	X	*Y*	*Z*
Direct Material	11	12	6
Direct Labour	7	9	12
Direct Expenses	4	3	2
Prime Cost	22	24	20
Indirect Works Expenses.	10	11	12
Works Cost	32	35	32
Indirect Administrative Expenses	8	6	5
Cost of Production	40	41	37
Selling and Distribution Expenses	18	16	15
Cost of Sales	58	57	52
Net Profit/Loss	7	−2	8
Sales Price	65	55	60

expenses are charged to X as opposed to Y and Z and, second, to make sure that all material, labour and expenses incurred during the period in which the costs are produced are reflected in one cost or another.

This second control, which should be ensured by the first, is often missing, especially in the case of such items as material wastage or idle labour time, which occurs during production, but which is not charged to any particular product. All managers must understand that accurate, and therefore reliable, costs depend upon the under-lying controls, and this must start from a realization that costing begins from the analysis of the profit and loss statement. To emphasize this point, the total of materials contained in X, Y and Z in the above illustration, plus those analysed for all other products, must be reconciled with the total material charged for the period in the profit and loss statement. It is the responsibility of managers to ensure that controls exist to verify the cost analysis and this will require an understanding of the nature of the analysis.

Direct Costs

In determining the analysis of expenses, it will be found that some items can be identified with the product produced, or service rendered, and some cannot. Expenses divided in this manner are termed "direct" and "indirect" respectively.

A direct expense, such as direct labour and direct material, is one which can be controlled as well as identified to a particular cost unit. In the case of direct material and direct labour, controls are required in the form of issue, return and transfer notes, job cards and time sheets which will trace each item of these expenses to the particular product, process or service. In these two areas an efficient system of material and labour control must presuppose a costing system and managers must look to their provision before relying upon the cost data presented.

Direct expenses, apart from direct labour and direct material, relate to items such as a royalty payable to a product designer or to supervisory labour which is incurred exclusively for the item being costed. All the remainder of the expenses are termed "indirect costs". Thus, in the illustration, out of a total cost of sales of 58, 57 and 52 for products X, Y and Z, only 22, 24 and 20 can be classified, if we ignore direct selling expenses such as salesmen's commission, as direct; the remainder 36, 33 and 32 are indirect expenses.

Indirect Costs

Indirect expenses are allocated on some suitable basis, but in order to determine this basis a series of estimates or guesses must take place. To illustrate the stages which are gone through in the preparation of indirect expense allocation, we shall examine how this may be done in the case of works expenses.

WORKS EXPENSE ALLOCATION SHEET

| | Total | | Cost Centres | | |
		1	2	3	4
Manager's Salary Indirect Wages Factory Rent etc.	}Guess I		Guess II		
	£200,000	£60,000	£70,000	£40,000	£30,000

Basis of allocation—Guess III = 120,000 Direct Labour hours for Cost Centre 1

We shall now examine this illustration in detail.

HEADING: Works Expense Allocation Sheet
It must be noted that, as works expenses are indirect, it will not be possible to identify the expense to the particular item produced. For this reason, it is necessary to estimate what the expenses will be

69

before the unit is costed so that an appropriate charge can be included to cover the anticipated expense.

TOTAL COLUMN: Forecast or Guess I
In the first place, an estimate must be made of the total expense under each head, e.g. managers' salaries, factory rent, rates, depreciation of plant and machinery, etc. The amounts will be found by reference to past data and future forecasts, much of which will very likely happen in the event, but the element of forecast or guess, and therefore the need for future verification when the facts are known, must never be ignored.

COST CENTRE ANALYSIS COLUMNS: Forecast or Guess II
These columns represent the analysis of the total figures for such items as rent, rates, etc., into locations which are considered necessary. This necessity is determined by the needs of management which in turn are governed by the way in which production passes through the factory. For instance, it may be found that not all production passes through all areas of the factory or uses the same plant and equipment. In this situation it would be incorrect to charge the same works expense to all products, irrespective of whether they use the same facilities.

By the use of cost centres, it is possible to divide the total expenses into the different areas through which production passes and, once these are established, each unit can be charged with the appropriate works expense. It should, however, be noted by management that the cost of a costing system will be greatly influenced by the number of cost centres created. The more cost centres there are the more calculations will be needed and the more clerical effort will be required. To determine whether or not a cost centre is needed a test can be taken to show the effect on the cost information of its inclusion or omission. If this is found to be negligible, a strong case will exist for the omission of that particular centre. The proliferation of cost centres without a real need or when they are no longer required, which can happen following a change in the production methods, should be avoided in the interests of cost reduction.

It should be noted in the illustration that the analysis of the total column into cost centres might require further breakdown than is shown in the example. For instance, the initial analysis could be a department of the factory and this could in turn be further analysed to an appropriate area within the department. This could be a machine or batch of machines. Whatever analysis is adopted, it must be noted that the basis of the breakdown will be an estimate and cannot be a totally accurate assessment. The basis used may be floor areas or the number of employees or whatever basis is found to be the most applicable. But in each case it must be recognized that the basis is arbitrary and complete accuracy is impossible.

The term "cost centre" is used here to denote the allocation of costs to a particular area to facilitate the building up of product costs. It must, however, be understood that a cost centre identifies expense to a particular location for the purpose of assisting management control and in the establishment of unit costs. All cost centres are eventually allocated to the unit of cost but they may be initially used to trace costs to a particular manager or location.

ALLOCATION BASIS: Guess III
Having arrived at the totals to be absorbed by products passing through each cost centre, it is now necessary to decide how to calculate the absorption per product. The allocation basis requires a fourth guess to be made.

To refer back to the example we shall assume that cost centre 1 has an amount of £60,000 allocated to it and this amount has to be passed to each product which goes through this cost centre. In arriving at the cost of a product passing through a cost centre, certain data will be known. These will include all the direct costs of material, labour and expenses which have gone into the product up to this stage of production. In addition to these values the quantities of material and the time of labour will also be known. In the case of a machine-controlled production cycle machine-times will also be known. Based on these data it is possible to select a reasonable basis which, in most cases, will be related to time. The reason for this choice is that most expenses such as salaries, rent, rates, insurance and depreciation are all influenced by time. The longer a product takes to pass through a cost centre, the more indirect expenses should be added. This means that the basis selected will either be direct labour hours or machine hours which relate to the particular cost-centre location, depending upon whether the production is labour- or machine-controlled.

To illustrate this point let us suppose that the production passing through cost centre 1 in the example is labour-controlled. The next step is to estimate how many labour hours will be expended in the production which will pass through the cost centre. This is forecast to be 120,000 direct labour hours, and so a works indirect expense rate of 50p is established for all units passing through the cost centre 1.

This examination of how cost centres are built up and how the expenses are absorbed into the unit costs highlights two important considerations for managers. First that indirect expenses added to costs are based on arbitrary allocation which cannot be made totally accurate, and second that the amount added to each cost is based on three forecasts, any of which may be wrong. The verification of these forecasts is a vital step in cost control.

The second forecast as to how to spread the total expenses over cost centres is one which once made must be accepted, but the forecast of total expenses under each head such as salaries, rent, etc., must be closely controlled during the period in which the actual expenditure takes place. Any over- or under-spending on these items will mean that the total cost shown will be incorrect thereby implying that the rate of recovery will be over- or under-sufficient.

The third guess, that of the basis of recovery, is perhaps the most sensitive forecast to change, and also the one most easily forgotten by those concerned with cost control. It should always be remembered that the recovery basis will be affected if more or less production takes place during the period. For instance, if in the previous example instead of 120,000 direct labour hours going into the production at the cost centre, a lack of orders reduces production to 60,000 direct labour hours, this will mean that only £30,000 indirect cost will be recovered (60,000 × 50p).

Alternatively, if production reached 180,000 direct labour hours, then £90,000 would be recovered (180,000 × 50p). The £30,000 under- and over-recovery would not be noticed unless a careful check was made to verify the allocation basis. Unless this is done at the end of the period management would be unaware of what was happening and as most of the expenditure allocated to the cost centre, such as salaries, rent, rates, insurance, etc., will remain fairly constant whatever the level of production, profits will be either reduced or increased by this £30,000 recovery difference.

Recovery of Administration, Sales and Transport Expenses

In the case of the other indirect expenses, such as general administration, selling and transport, the rate of recovery is often arrived at by applying an arbitrary rate to all products. For example, take a case where sales during the next twelve months are estimated to be £1,000,000; it is estimated that direct material, direct labour and direct expenses will amount to 55 per cent of this with works expenses at £100,000; and that administration, sales and transport expenses will be £52,000, £130,000 and £65,000 respectively. In such a case the calculation of the absorption rates for administration sales, and distribution will be as follows:

		£	
Prime Cost (Direct Material, Labour & Expenses)		550,000	(55 per cent of sales)
Works Expenses		100,000	
Works Cost		650,000	
Administration Expenses		52,000	
		702,000	
	£		
Selling	130,000		
Distribution . .	65,000	195,000	

In this situation, administration, selling and transport expenses may be calculated as percentages of works cost. These are 8, 20 and 10 per cent respectively, and these percentages can be used whenever a cost is being prepared. Once a works cost is known, the relevant percentage can be added to account for these later indirect expenses.

This somewhat arbitrary way of absorbing these other indirect expenses owes much to the historical fact that works expenses were in earlier days by far the largest area of indirect expense. However, in recent years this situation has in many cases been reversed and there is a real need for a more analytical approach to overhead recovery in these later stages. This is especially true of selling expense which has grown in most enterprises into a major item. These comments regarding the absorption of indirect expenses apply to a large extent to the service industries and it is of very real importance for management in these industries to insist on a greater attempt to control and identify such expenses to services and/or to management control locations.

Indirect Expense Allocation: General

All managers should be aware of the fact that costs below the prime cost point are based largely on forecasts which require very close control and verification. In certain cases, for instance if one is part way through a control period, verification will be impossible for some time. For this reason, many costs presented to managers are pending agreement and if action is planned based on such data, care should be taken before committing an enterprise to a change in policy until the data have been agreed. This point is becoming more and more important as the proportion of costs included as indirect expenses increases.

This increase is a natural development in a technological age in which a large number of products pass through common processes and skilled labour and special materials are replaced by automated machines and substitute materials. The growth of market-orientated enterprises also increases the expenditure under the selling head and this is found often to be compensated by a reduction in prime costs.

Full Historical Costing

The method of costing which has been described above is referred to as "full historical". This name denotes the fact that all forms of expenditure are charged or allocated to each unit of cost and that the expense in each case is based on its cost when it was incurred with no reference to possible changes in price if the product or service is to be produced in the future. The adoption of an historical basis in assessing expenses can have a very misleading effect if the costs are required to tell management whether or not it is worth while to continue the production of a particular product. The difficulty of changing prices is particularly relevant in the case of materials whose prices may vary enormously over fairly short periods of time.

The point for managers to note in this respect is that they must clearly state the purpose for which they require the cost of a product or service. Costing is a very versatile and adaptable technique and, despite its definitions and jargon, costs can be prepared in many different ways to assist the varying needs of management.

Summary

The following summary of guidance is presented to assist non-financial managers wishing to use costing information:

1 In every business a costing system of any kind whatsoever must be preceded by the implementation of physical controls, namely labour control and material control. This is not just true of manufacturing businesses. Material control is very applicable in the retail or factoring industry and labour control is vital in every labour-dependent service industry.

2 In setting up a costing system the unit of cost must be decided. This must follow the needs of management, and the manager concerned with the control of the financial information must consult with all levels of management on this point. It may be found that the

unit of cost will not be the finished unit of output but a stage in the production cycle such as a process. It should be noted that the more detailed the analysis is, the greater will be the cost of its provision. Moreover, apart from the product or service being the unit of cost, managers may wish to analyse costs into locations for expense control. Such location costs are referred to as cost centres and are eventually absorbed into the product or service cost.

3 Having determined the unit of cost, it is necessary to decide which expenses are direct and which are indirect. The direct costs are those which can be identified with the unit of cost and the indirect expenses are those which will require some basis of absorption to allocate them to the individual units. Whatever basis of allocation is decided all indirect expenses will be added to the units of cost based on a series of forecasts or guesses.

These will require continual checking to see that such forecasts are in agreement with what expenses are actually incurred. It should be noted in the case of overhead expense recovery that this may entail the setting up of cost centres. The number of these will greatly influence the volume of clerical work within the costing system and it is suggested that managers should question the need for each cost centre so as to ensure that the cost of the costing system is kept within bounds.

4 Because of the forecast basis upon which indirect expenses are charged to the units of cost, the higher the proportion of direct cost to total costs, the more reliable will be the information presented. It is therefore in the interest of those reviewing costs to make sure that wherever possible an item is treated as direct, as opposed to indirect. There are certain border-line examples which might fit under either head such as a foreman who supervises the production of one particular unit of output. This expense might be treated as indirect expense as it refers to a salary, but it will add to the reliability of the unit cost if it is included among the direct expenses. The need to raise the proportion of direct to indirect expenses in order to improve the reliability of the costing data should be borne in mind by all managers and the division of expenses under the two heads should be reviewed by all those concerned with the information and not left to the decision of those who are presenting it.

5 Management must clearly set out the purpose of the costing data which they wish to be presented to them. They must be aware that the data may be adapted to their different needs and this is especially true when cost information is required to assist decisions involving the future policies of the enterprise. In this connection, special care must be taken in the areas which are highly subject to inflationary pressures such as direct material and sales prices.

MARGINAL COSTING

An alternative way of presenting cost information is known as "marginal costing". This method takes into consideration the fact that expenses, as well as being direct and indirect to the location or unit being costed, may be classified as variable or fixed. This concept of expense stems from economic theory which refers to the ambition of the entrepreneur to expand his business at the point where the additional cost of producting one more unit equals the additional revenue from selling it.

The reason for this situation is that as more and more units are produced the pressure of supply and demand upon each item of expense will eventually cause the cost to increase. Material suppliers will realize that the demand for their products gives them an opportunity to put up their prices and the same situation will occur in the case of labour and overheads. It will also be found as more units are produced which require to be sold that it will be necessary in the end to reduce the sales prices to ensure their disposal.

This increase in cost and reduction in revenue will eventually bring about the circumstances in which the additional cost of producing one more unit will be exactly the same as the additional revenue from selling it and it will no longer be in the interest of the business to continue to operate.

Adaptation of Marginal Theory

This theory of economics has been adapted by accountants in presenting cost information and this is what has grown into the technique known as marginal costing. It must first be noted that this technique is adapted from the basic economic theory in terms of the immediate limited future. No intention exists to present marginal costing data as a basis to examine long periods ahead for any enterprise. At most it is suitable for the next twelve months and even then the basis on which expenses are divided should be verified at frequent intervals.

The technique of marginal costing considers expenses in the light of present output and divides them into those which are in this context variable and those which are fixed. The variable expenses might be termed those additional costs of producing one more product or rendering one more service. Such expenses will include the direct material and direct labour costs which would not be incurred if the product or service were not produced. It would also include items of variable expense such as the salesman's commission or a royalty paid to the designer of the product and paid at the rate of so much per unit produced. On the other hand, during the immediate period ahead, certain expenses will be seen to remain unchanged or fixed. Such items include rent, rates, insurance and administrative salaries.

This view of expenses is one which is applicable only over a short period ahead. It certainly does not apply in the long term and the economist who is concerned with long-term trends does not fit his theory into such narrow parameters. He sees all expense as variable in the long run. Rent will be increased, rateable values will alter as a result of the prosperity of the enterprise and salaries will rise because of the demands of those employed in a thriving business.

The important point for the manager to understand from this review of the theory of marginal costing is that the data presented are based on the immediate situation within the business. The idea that certain expenses are directly variable with the volume of units produced or services rendered is true only within certain recognized limits. For instance, during the next twelve months and with production remaining at a particular level certain expenses will be directly variable and some will remain fixed. Outside these limits, however, the relationship between variable and fixed expenses will change. Material prices and labour rates may alter and, although fixed expenses may be known over the short period immediately ahead, to assume that they will remain unchanged over a longer period can be very misleading to those being presented with marginal cost data. It is essential that managers should recognize the limited nature of marginal costing.

Marginal Cost Analysis

On page 78 we show a conventional full cost and see how this will be adapted if it is presented as a marginal cost.

The marginal cost of product X is 33p as opposed to 76p, which is its full cost. It will be noted that within the marginal cost only those expenses which vary with the units produced are included. So we find direct material, labour and expenses and variable indirect expenses added together to form the marginal cost.

It will be seen in this example that all direct costs are also variable but all indirect costs are not fixed. This situation may not always be found to exist and certainly in the case of direct labour it would be unusual for a business to dispose of its direct labour, which would in many cases be skilled labour, as soon as production failed to reach a predetermined level. This problem of variables not responding exactly to the theory reinforces the proposition that this technique must be viewed with a fairly critical mind.

			Product X	
			Full Cost	Marginal Cost
			p	p
Direct Material	. . . .		10	10
Direct Labour	. . . . . .		8	8
Direct Expenses	. . . . .		2	2
			—	—
Prime cost	. . . .		20	20
Works expenses				
Fixed	. . . .	12		
Variable	. . . .	4	16	4
			—	—
Works cost	. . . . . .		36	
Administration Expenses				
Fixed	. . . .	10		
Variable	. . . .	—	10	—
			—	
Cost of production	. . . . . .		46	
Selling expenses				
Fixed	. . . .	15		
Variable	. . . .	8	23	8
		—		
Transport expenses:				
Fixed	. . . .	6		
Variable	. . . .	1	7	1
		—	—	—
Cost of sales	. . . .		76	33
Net profit	. . . .		9	
Margin or contribution			—	52
			—	—
Sales price	. . . .		85	85

Variable and Fixed Expenses

There are indeed certain expenses which follow exactly the production patterns, such as direct material or a royalty payable per unit produced. But many so-called variable expenses, such as direct labour or a jig cost, which is written off over the number of products it is presumed will be produced with its aid, are in fact unlikely to cease if the volume of production stops. The problem of determining which expenses are fixed and which are variable has created a great deal of theoretical debate which has not assisted the understanding of the technique.

Expressions such as "semi-variable" or "fixed-variable" denoting the fact that some expenses consist of a variable part and a fixed part are examples of these. It is stressed that much of this theory becomes of academic interest only if the transient nature of defining expenses as fixed or variable is recognized. It should be noted at this stage that it is becoming more and more common to bring all direct expenses into the marginal cost of a unit and this point is developed later in this chapter.

Having recognized that certain expenses can be classified over the short period ahead as either fixed or variable it is possible not only to construct unit costs as illustrated in the previous example on the basis of marginal costs but also to review the revenue and expense of the entire business and divide it in this manner.

The Contribution

It will be noted in the previous illustration that the difference between the marginal cost and the sales price of product X is termed the "contribution" or "margin". This difference is not the same as net profit, but it indicates the amount which this product contributes towards the expenses not included in this cost, namely the fixed expenses of the enterprise.

This view of income and expenditure is one which is highly relevant to managerial decisions in that it recognizes that, until the fixed expenses of the enterprise have been covered, no profit whatsoever has been made. It also leads to the recognition that, as many of those expenses are contracted for over periods of twelve months or even more, the idea that a profit is made in a fraction of this time, like a month, is misleading and can lead to an incorrect interpretation of the profitability of the concern.

Further, it can be argued that, as fixed expenses such as rent, rates, salaries, insurance, etc., are of a period nature, these should never be carried forward as the cost of stocks in their different stages of production. This argument states that such expenses should be written off or charged in the final accounts for the period to which they relate and no attempt should be made to carry them forward as part of the cost of stock.

The Break-even Chart

To illustrate this view of the income and expense of an entire business let us examine what is termed a "break-even chart" (see Fig. 6).

This is the more usual manner of showing expenses and income to illustrate the adaptation of marginal costing principles to the enterprise as a whole. The term "break even" refers to the point

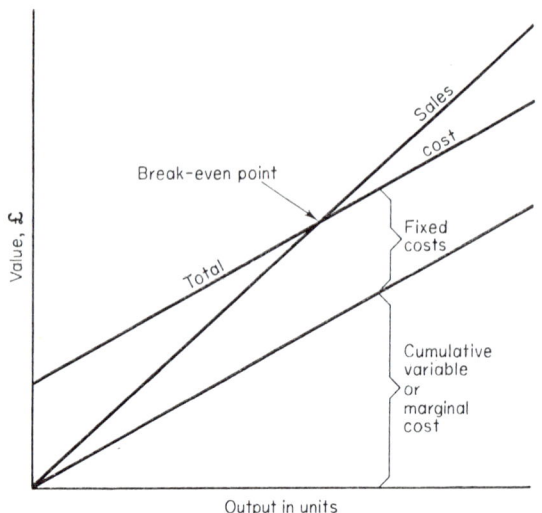

FIGURE 6 **Break-even chart**

expressed in either terms of sales or production at which the contribution is sufficient to meet all fixed expenses for the period under review.

To illustrate this situation, let us examine a one-product business with a margin or contribution per unit of 50p, and a total fixed expense over the next twelve months of £600,000. The break-even point for this period will be calculated by dividing the fixed expenses (£600,000) by the contribution per unit (50p) and the answer (1,200,000) is the number of units which must be produced and sold to cover fixed expenses, that is break even. If the sales price per unit is £3, the sales value of the break-even point will be £3,600,000. If production and sales can be expressed in time it would also be possible to express the break-even point in this manner. For example, if the business produced and sold 200,000 units per month, the break-even point would occur at the end of month 6.

An alternative way of presenting a break-even chart is set out in Fig. 70.

This alternative is now superseded by the first method shown as the latter sets out more clearly how the contribution first goes towards covering the fixed expenses and then at the break-even point the contribution becomes all profit.

Break-even Analysis

In reviewing the break-even chart it must be recognized that the lines are drawn on certain assumptions which make the chart

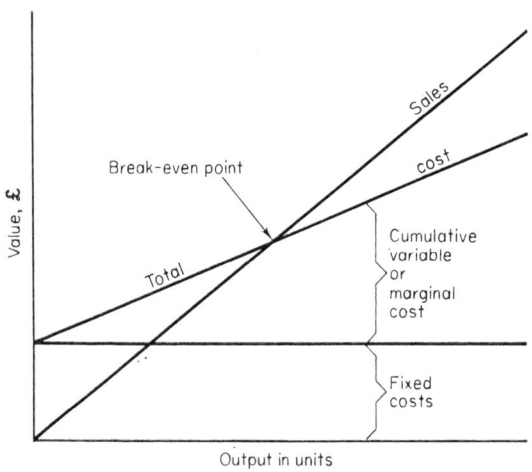

FIGURE 7 **Break-even chart—alternative version**

correct only under certain circumstances. The picture presented in the break-even chart is correct only if the production capacity is used within certain maximum and minimum limits. Within these limits the break-even point and the view of the income and expenditure set out on the chart are correct. However, if the capacity fell below or rose above these limits, the lines up to and beyond these points would be somewhat different.

For instance, it would be most unlikely that direct labour, no longer required if production did not reach the minimum point, would be dismissed immediately. In these circumstances, it is likely that labour would be kept on for a period of time awaiting the possibility of future production. Such labour would then become a fixed expense and the fixed expense would increase correspondingly. Similarly, if production exceeds the maximum point, it is likely that the cost of labour per unit might increase because of the need to pay overtime rates to fulfil the production demands. It might also be found that the increased usage of material caused by the additional production created a situation in which suppliers decided to increase their prices.

It is therefore seen that if a business achieves a production below or beyond the set capacity this might affect considerably the construction of the break-even chart and also the view of the profitability of the business given by the diagram. It should be clearly understood that a break-even chart and the data it contains are applicable only in relation to a restricted capacity usage as discussed

81

and also for the limited period of time described in the title, e.g. "Break-even Chart for X Ltd, for twelve months". One danger of marginal costing and the presentation of break-even charts in practice is that it induces managers to believe that expenses and income can be viewed in this manner over long periods ahead and the amount and proportion of variable and fixed expenses to total costs will remain unchanged irrespective of the volume of output and the lapse of time. It is hoped that the above explanation will arm all managers against the glib approach to marginal costing which is so widespread in modern business.

Expense/Income Changes and the Break-even Point

The reader is advised to study the break-even chart and note the effect of changes in fixed and variable expenses upon the break-even point. It is in fact quite possible for an enterprise to break even at one level of production and on increasing the fixed and/or variable expenses to find it has to obtain a second break even. This situation is illustrated below:

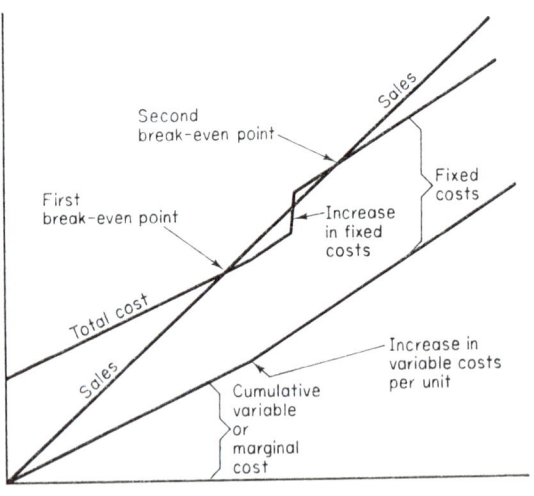

FIGURE 8

Contribution Comparison

Having examined the language of marginal costing let us now see how we can use this technique for managerial decisions.

In the first place we shall examine a situation which might exist in a business producing or rendering a series of products or services. The marginal costs of these products or services are as follows:

Products/Services

	A	B	C	D	E
Marginal cost	10	8	9	14	6
Contribution	2	1	4	6	2
Sales price	12	9	13	20	8

It will be noted that the contributions, unlike net profits, are calculated before deducting fixed expenses and so it would be incorrect to take these as a measure of profitability. This is especially the case where the products vary in their time of production or depend in varying degrees upon some other factor such as material usage or value. It is nevertheless most important for managers to form some basis of comparing contribution so as to rank products in order of profitability. To achieve this object it is necessary for management to decide which factor limits the enterprise, and use this as the basis by which the margins or contributions can be compared. It is then possible to define the profit objective of management as having to maximize contribution per the limiting factor of the enterprise.

Limiting Factors

This limiting factor will depend upon the business, but in many cases it might be the sales which can be obtained for its output or again it could be its production capacity if it can sell all it can produce. Both these limits can be converted into time either as direct labour or machine hours by converting the sales or production into labour or machine hours needed to meet the limited sales volume or production capacity. Another limiting factor in some businesses might be material usage when there is a shortage of the raw material which goes into the production of each unit. The limiting factor is therefore the factor which limits the number of units produced or the volume of services rendered. Once this has been determined margins can be ranked in the order of the maximum contribution per limiting factor.

So far, limiting factors have been mentioned which would apply to the entire or a large part of the enterprise. However, it is often found useful to measure the contribution per limiting factor of products which pass through a particular production process in which the production is severely limited by some local factor such as a particular type of skilled operative or of machine tool. In such circumstances the contribution per local limiting factor could be measured and once the order of merit was established the sales mix could be decided in the light of these findings. An illustration of this use of limiting factors is set out below:

BELON LTD

Belon Ltd sells five product lines. The five products are manufactured on a bank of 60 power presses, any of which may be used on each of the five products. It is estimated that each press can produce 40 hours' work per week.

The data relating to the products are as follows:

Product	Total cost	Variable cost	Selling price	No. of press hrs	Estimated demand per month
			Per unit		
	£	£	£		
A	26	20	30	3	1,400
B	35	28	40	6	1,900
C	72	52	85	7	300
D	20	15	30	5	1,800
E	18	14	30	4	600

Fixed costs amount to £23,400 per month.
What combination of products would produce the maximum profit?

SOLUTION

The objective is to develop the best mix of products. This involves maximizing the limiting factor which is in this case the number of machine hours. It should be noted that the total cost, in this technique, is irrelevant, and is probably even misleading.

Product	Selling price per unit	Variable cost	Contribution	Hrs req	Contribution per unit of time	Best product
	£	£	£			
A	30	20	10	3	3·3	3
B	40	28	12	6	2·0	5
C	85	52	33	7	4·7	1
D	30	15	15	5	3·0	4
E	30	14	16	4	4·0	2

To maximize the profits based on 9,600 hours capacity per month produce:

Product	Demand	Produce	Hrs		Total hrs	Contribution £
C	300	300	7	=	2,100	9,900
E	600	600	4	=	2,400	9,600
A	1,400	1,400	3	=	4,200	13,860
D	1,800	180	5	=	900	2,700
					9,600 hrs	36,060
					Less fixed costs	23,400
					Net profit	12,660

84

Contribution per Limiting Factor

In a medium-sized organization or within a section of a large enterprise, it may be possible to determine an average ideal contribution per limiting factor by dividing the fixed expenses for the following period, plus the required net profit, by the appropriate limiting factor. To illustrate this situation, we shall examine the following data:

A LTD

	£
Capital employed	1,000,000
Profit on capital employed before taxation	15 per cent
Fixed expense for next year	750,000

The limiting factor is sales, which converted into the production capacity to meet this represents 1,800,000 direct labour hours.

To compute the *ideal* contribution per direct labour hour, the following calculation is necessary:

	£
Net profit required	150,000
(15 per cent of £1,000,000)	
Fixed expenses	750,000
	900,000

$$\text{Ideal contribution per limiting factor} = \frac{900,000}{1,800,000} = £0.50 \text{ per direct labour hour}$$

Where it is possible to determine an ideal contribution per limiting factor as set out above, it is then possible to check each product produced or service rendered and the sales prices of these items to see whether or not their individual contributions per limiting factor measure up to the computed figure. The technique can then be used to assess the pricing policy of the enterprise.

Product Service Comparison

It should be especially noted that contribution comparisons can be used just as readily by non-manufacturing organizations. In such cases the limiting factor might be shelf space in a retail shop or consultant's time in the case of a management consultant. Knowing the ideal contribution will enable management to review its products or services and to arrange its sales mix to maximize the profitability of the enterprise. The selection of the limiting factor will depend entirely upon the particular business, and care will be required in its

85

selection. It may be found in the larger business that the factor will vary from area to area of the firm and in such cases separate calculations will be required.

Marginal Costing and Management Decisions

The determination of the contribution per limiting factor to break even and that required to attain the required return on capital enables management to review sales prices of products to see whether they provide an adequate profit. It can, however, be argued that in the case of severe competition a product that can be sold at anything above its marginal cost is at least making some contribution to fixed expenses. This would not happen if the item remained unsold and, based on this reasoning, sales prices at just above the marginal cost might be justified during periods of severe competition. This knowledge on which to base price reductions might also be useful in the case of a business with surplus production capacity but no demand for their products at the normal sales prices above a particular sales volume. In such cases, management with the data provided by marginal costing might decide to reduce the sales price and thus increase the sales once the maximum point has been reached. This would enable fuller use to be made of the production capacity. Such a reduction would not adversely affect profits as at that point the break-even would have been achieved plus the forecasted profits of the enterprise, and so any revenue in excess of the marginal cost would be of benefit. It should be noted that any use of marginal costing in this manner would have to be done in conjunction with the marketing function. Such marketing techniques as loss-leaders and brand-label changes owe much to such co-operation.

Marginal Costing Summary

These, therefore, are the techniques which can be made available to management by the use of marginal costing and the main features of this system are set out below:

1 Marginal costing reduces and simplifies the analysis necessary to determine unit, process or service cost. In this system only variable expenses are allocated to the cost units as fixed expenses are left in total. It therefore reduces the clerical work involved in preparing costs and should enable the data to be presented that much earlier.

2 The division of expenses into variable and fixed, which must

presuppose any marginal costing system, will require decisions to be made. In these decisions theory must be tempered with practical considerations, the major one being that in the long term no expense will vary directly with production and that no expense will remain fixed indefinitely. With these two facts in mind any long-drawn-out discussions as to whether or not an item is to be classed as fixed or variable loses much of its point.

It should, however, be remembered that unless a fair proportion of the costs are classed as variable, say over 30 per cent, the resultant analysis will be too little to give a reasonable indication of the unit cost and the resultant margin or contribution will be difficult to use in management decision-making.

3 The determination of the contribution and from this the break-even point provides management with a new concept of profit, income and expense. It enables managers to see the need to cover fixed expenses before any profit whatsoever can be really earned. It also begins to highlight for them the significance of production hold-ups. For example, the cost of a strike or of waiting for material or of a shop closing for half a day is not the cost of the labour or material involved in production. It is the cost of the fixed expense which will continue but will not be recovered because of the failure to produce the units or render the service. This view of expense and income, which can be seen in the break-even chart, is of real signi-ficance to managers and will concentrate their control in the key areas of variable expenses, sales volume and prices and fixed expenses in total. If these items are kept to the amount forecast, the break-even point will be reached and the desired profit will be achieved.

4 An understanding of the contribution per product leads to a recognition of the limiting factor which will again concentrate the attention of management on determining first what is the limiting factor of the enterprise or each part of it, and second which product or mix of products will maximize profitability. This understanding of the limiting factor and relating contribution to this is a vital step in understanding profit measurement and for this reason has a growing application as a financial technique.

It is also a useful measure in examining sales prices and, in the case of a new product, checking the suggested sales price with that which would be arrived at by adding to the estimated marginal cost the ideal contribution per limiting factor. It has therefore an application in the area of pricing.

5 The information available from marginal costing provides data which may prove useful both in periods of severe competition and when sales do not take up all the production capacity available. These two situations were discussed in detail above and possible

solutions may be found with the assistance of marginal costing data.

Marginal Costing: General Conclusions

There has been much criticism of marginal costing and most of this stems from the temptation to over-simplify the data presented. It is suggested that the need to verify continually that variable expenses have varied constantly through the period, and that fixed expenses are in accordance with the forecasts, must be recognized by all managers and the underlying control must be verified. However, the need for such verification is equally necessary in a system of full costing and this cannot therefore be classed as a special need of marginal costing.

The major problem of marginal costing is that certain expenses which are direct to a particular product may not be a variable expense and for this reason will not be classed as part of the marginal cost. This will mean that the margin or contribution for such a product will be inflated as certain directly related expenses will not be included in the cost. An example of such an expense is depreciation of a special-purpose machine tool which is used in the production of one product. Depreciation is a fixed expense which will not theoretically be included within the marginal cost. This problem may be overcome by ignoring the theory of marginal costing and including such direct expenses as part of the marginal cost. In such cases, marginal costing becomes what might be termed direct costing, which includes all variable cost plus any other direct expenses of the particular product or service.

CONCLUSION

Management has asked for analysis and the two costing systems outlined in this chapter are what have been provided. It should be remembered that costing is analysis of what has happened and when it is adopted to forecast future situations the information presented must await confirmation from future events.

The need for continual control and verification has been emphasized throughout this chapter and it is most important that all those making use of cost data should be willing to ask questions and continue to ask them until the significance of the data presented is thoroughly understood.

4   *Comparative Controls*

There is a basic need for comparison whenever financial information relating to past or present events is presented. This need is found in the expressions "what happened last time", or "let's see the estimate". To the seeker of such comparison the need is obvious. He wants to measure whether or not in the event the business, or whatever part of it he is looking at, is progressing satisfactorily.

The measure of progress may be as basic as whether or not it is doing as well as last time or last year or whether the actual cost of a product is more or less than an estimate which was calculated taking into consideration every conceivable inefficiency. On the other hand, the comparison may be based on the most detailed analysis of future trends of income and expenses, but whatever the basis may be, every manager presented with financial data seeks comparisons.

BUDGETARY CONTROL AND STANDARD COSTING

For this reason the two formalized techniques which have been developed to assist management in this respect are often found to be present in part in enterprises which are not aware of their existence. Having been created in response to management's real need, such systems are worth far more than if they had been formally introduced without understanding or request on the part of management.

The two techniques which form the basis of comparative financial information are budgetary control and standard costing. Budgetary control is concerned with the translation of the plans and schemes of the entire business into financial terms, whilst standard costing limits its comparison to the area of cost control. This latter technique is sometimes incorrectly introduced to managers as an alternative system of costing. This is not so. It is an addition to any method of costing as it is concerned with the comparison of actual costs with pre-set standards and the analysis of the difference between these two sets of figures.

The need for comparison in costing is possibly the most obvious area to managers. It stems from a need to know whether or not the cost of producing a service or product is in line with the forecast and this may seem a more immediate management requirement than the translation of policies into financial terms undertaken in budgetary control. For this reason, the earliest demands for comparison may arise in the costing area. However, despite the way in which comparison needs may grow within the enterprise, we shall examine the two major techniques in the accepted order of, first, budgetary control and, second, standard costing.

BUDGETARY CONTROL

In the first place budgetary control, from a corporate viewpoint, is the translation of policy into financial terms, so that the effect of it can be seen in terms of how much will be invested in fixed assets, working capital and outside investment (as shown in the key diagram) if we adopt the policy and how much, if any, additional permanent funds will be required to undertake this investment. Together with this financial translation of the investment policy there will also be a forecast made of the return on such investment by means of a calculation of the ensuing profit or loss. Having established these forecasts, it will then be necessary to set up the second part of budgetary control which is to progress actual performance against these.

Presentation for Management

This overall view of budgetary control could be expressed in terms of a profit and loss statement and balance sheet set out for the period ahead and broken down into convenient comparative points such as months or quarters. Budgetary control in this form will enable top management to review the policy progress of the enterprise and the financial function will have data with which to calculate the return on capital employed. It does, however, leave the managers who are concerned with the day-to-day control of the business with very little useful data. They do not see life or their spheres of influence in terms of profit and loss statements and balance sheets. They see

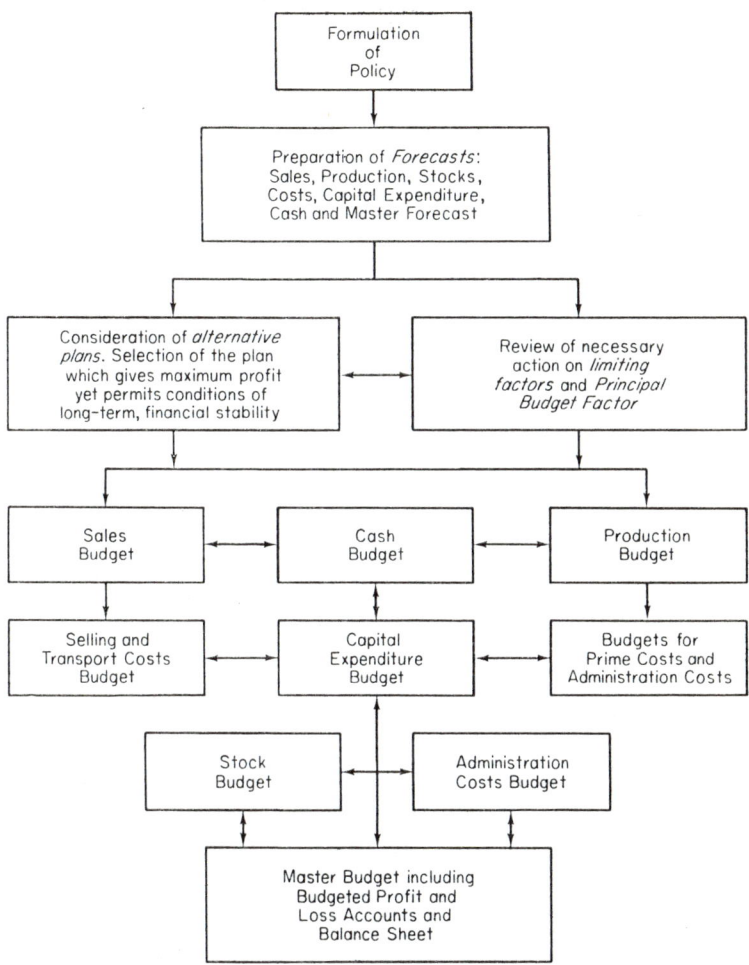

FIGURE 9 **Budgetary control procedure diagram**

day-to-day control in terms of departmental or section targets against actual expense and income, and material usage and labour efficiency forecasts against actual performance. But most of all they see comparison for management purposes in human terms. Who is responsible for what? What is his target? Has he achieved it? Of course, it will all eventually form part of a profit and loss statement and balance sheet, but in the meantime control can only be ensured through human involvement and understanding. This is the first point to note in budgetary control. It is based on a pyramid view of information with the apex being the profit and loss statement and balance sheet and the base being management control and involvement.

The Conflict of Presentation

The need to express budgeting in terms of management control must be recognized by those introducing the techniques. The differences between the immediate need to translate the policy of the business into budgeted final accounts and to compare these with actual data throughout future periods has been known to conflict with the pragmatic needs of management in their day-to-day control of the enterprise. This conflicting interest is one which concerns the presentation and not the content of the data, but as this is fundamental to the acceptance of this technique it must be taken into consideration.

It must be remembered that the success of budgetary control depends upon the co-operation of managers at all levels and in practice it is found that, where there is a choice in priority between providing useful data to either senior or junior management, the system is more likely to benefit the enterprise if the latter level is first satisfied.

Control Procedure

A budgetary-control procedure diagram is shown on page 91. This sets out the stages in producing a system of budgetary control and these are explained in the following paragraphs.

FORMATION OF POLICY

Budgetary control is based on a corporate policy and this is the first benefit to be derived from this technique. Management must have a policy. Unless this is present the technique becomes totally unworkable as each function, viz. sales, production and finance, will have to develop its own policies which, if they cannot be reconciled one with the other, will produce a situation of anarchy. In formulating the policy the top management will divide their thinking into short-, medium- and long-term plans and the financial forecasts developed from their plans will be shaped to meet these three stages.

In thinking around future plans there will be a certain constraining factor or factors depending upon whether one is concerned with short- or long-term forecasting. For instance, a company providing a particular type of service might find demand limited for this service

92

over the immediate future period although this might be changed over a longer period by developing the demand through marketing techniques. It will be noted that this limitation can be related back to the limiting factor which we discussed under marginal costing. It should be noted that in deciding future policy top management must be well aware of the limiting factor, or as it is termed in this connection, the "principal budget factor", which will circumscribe their thinking.

However, such limitation should not prevent management from allowing themselves in their development of policy to explore every possible area of future progress. It will normally be found that whatever the principal budget factor, whether it is sales, production, raw material, skilled labour or financial resources, it will be expressed in terms of a particular sales volume. This forecast will take into consideration the limiting factor and once again marginal costing data may prove useful in the setting of the forecast. For example, a proposed sales volume in a particular mix can be translated into its marginal cost and from this the adequacy or otherwise of the resulting contribution can be examined.

The process of policy-making so as to link this with producing a financial budget may be summarized as follows:

(*a*) Recognize the principal budget factor in the near, medium and long distance ahead.

(*b*) Prepare, in outline, short-, medium- and long-term policies.

(*c*) Experiment with alternative budgets around the policies prepared for the future periods.

(*d*) In the light of each budget examine the return on the capital employed to assist in measuring the profitability of the enterprise if the policies are carried out. In this connection it must be recognized that management is more concerned with stable profits than immediate gains followed by future losses.

SUPPLEMENTARY BUDGETS

It is stressed that the top management of a business wishing to implement budgetary control cannot delegate policy-making to the individual function heads. It is also important to note that such policy-making must be specific enough for no doubt to be left as to the limits within which management will be working. The overall forecasts presented within the policy will then require the preparation of detailed supplementary budgets by the lower management levels.

These detailed budgets will take the form of translating policy into terms of day-to-day management control. For these to be understood we shall examine the main categories of these forecasts.

Sales

Once the principal budget factor has been determined and taken into consideration in establishing the policy the sales-mix volume referred to above becomes the limiting factor around which all expense budgets are constructed. It will be expressed in terms of numbers of units to be sold in each category but this will need to be broken down into the needs of the marketing function. Examples of this analysis would be sales in each division or in each sales area or in sales by hire purchase as opposed to normal credit or cash transactions. Whatever breakdown is felt necessary, the need will be served by a rearrangement of the overall sales budget. In all cases it will be found that the budgets will be constructed around management responsibility.

Production

Having established the sales budget, it is then possible to construct a production budget taking into account the forecasted volume and mix of sales including the stock levels which have been budgeted by top management. The production budget will be analysed into its several parts, namely material, labour and expenses. These again will require breaking down under individual management responsibilities. The details obtained from the individual production budgets may be formed into budgeted costs of the units or services produced.

Capital Expenditure

The forming of policy regarding future sales will determine the trading pattern of the organization for the period ahead, and this in turn will dictate the fixed assets (i.e. capital expenditure) which will be required. The capital-expenditure budget will not simply reflect the immediate future trading obtained from short-term plans but must also take account of medium- and long-term policies. For this reason, capital-expenditure budgeting is much less flexible when once put into motion than other forms of expenditure and requires very careful linking with the trading pattern of the enterprise. The link between the sales and production patterns and the fixed-asset investment required to meet the future trading needs must be fully understood by all managers. Such investment may occur in many different areas within the establishment and it is necessary that everyone concerned with the use and provision of fixed assets should be fully consulted about the forecasted amounts which are proposed to be invested. Once again capital-expenditure budgets will be constructed so as to bring out individual managers' responsibilities and their information needs.

Expense Budgets, including Administration, Sales and Transport

These individual expense budgets must await the preparation of sales, production and capital-expenditure budgets before they can be compiled. Some items of expense may be of a fixed nature such as rents, rates, salaries, etc., but many will vary to some extent with production and/or sales and even with the capital-expenditure investment and must therefore await the preparation of these primary budgets.

In these expense areas it is vital that the overall expense under each head, such as administration, selling, transport and financial, is analysed to particular management responsibility. This analysis requires great care so that the budgets produced are relevant to the needs of such control. In this connection, the need for care in determining managers' responsibility to influence the expenses included is a vital feature of such budget preparation.

Cash Budgets

Having prepared the budgets for each item of expense, income stocks and capital expenditure, the effect will be that all items which enter into the profit and loss statement and balance sheet will have been forecast for the period or periods ahead with the sole exception of the cash balance on the balance sheet and the balances relating to people or organizations from whom or to whom money is owing or owed: i.e. debtors and creditors.

To compute the budgeted final accounts in these areas, it is necessary therefore to compute the cash effect of the budgets so far produced. It will be found that cash payments do not always coincide with expenditure in the relevant expense budgets and cash receipts will not always occur in accordance with the income budget. These differences between receipts and payment and income and expenditure are explained by the credit taken and received within business transactions. It will be seen when we examine the cash budget in detail that the statement may reveal that, however attractive a policy may be to management, it is beyond the day-to-day cash resources of the business or that to attain the targets set an overdraft facility will be required from their bankers.

Profit and Loss Statement and Balance Sheet Budgets

As previously pointed out, each budget will form a part of the final accounts and, once all the budgets have been prepared, a complete budgeted profit and loss statement and balance sheet will be available. The period for which such final accounts will be prepared will depend upon the type of budgeting which has been undertaken. Whether this is short-, medium- or long-term, it is considered advisable that an attempt should be made to produce final accounts to cover the immediate quarterly periods ahead for, say, twelve months, and at least one annual set of final accounts for the two years from the date of the forecast. This will ensure a disciplined approach to policy-making and will give experience to managers in the technique of forecasting.

The Organization of Budgetary Control Presentation

Experience shows that not only is little attention, if any, given to the organization of budgetary control, but also that this technique is perhaps the most under-used and misunderstood of all management information procedures. It is suggested that there is a connection between these two experiences. Too often the comment from managers when discussing budgetary control is that it is data used to check on managers in a negative manner. Such remarks as "Good differences between forecast and actual are ignored, bad ones are chased mercilessly", or "The budget in the first place is unreal and anyway I don't know how it was set" are commonly heard. Each time the cause for this dissatisfaction has been found to stem from the organization of budgetary control.

Budgetary control in most cases is found to be part of the financial function and, as such, the preparation and presentation of the information comes under the control of the financial manager. In practice this has been found to have several disadvantages. The first is that, as the financial function has a vested interest in producing one budget, namely the profit and loss statement and balance sheet or master budget, other budgets may become subservient to this.

A concentration upon producing the master budget may lead to a situation in which other expense and income budgets are prepared more to fit in with the master budget than to coincide with the sphere of control of particular managers. The result of this is that managers may be issued with budgets showing income and expense for which they are termed responsible but over which they may find they have little or no control whatsoever. Anyone with any experience of presenting managers with information, some of which is and some of which is not relevant, will know that a blend of this nature produces one result—all such information is ignored after the first glance. It is vital that financial data presented to managers is relevant to their needs and this is especially true when the information may be a personal reflection upon the competence of the particular manager to control his area of the enterprise.

The second reason why the financial function may not be the one best suited to control the presentation of budgetary control is their very competence to do so. This may sound like a contradiction, but in fact the translation of a policy into detailed budgets involves considerable work and effort. If the task is to be done correctly, each subsidiary budget requires detailed discussions and full understanding on the part of those managers whose duty it will be to control them. Too often it is found that the task of producing budgets is so onerous to the financial function that short cuts are looked for which include in some cases arriving at budgets and deciding areas of control without the necessary consultation. This is not to say that the budgets are inaccurate. In many cases, budget information is not difficult to determine from data available within the financial function but consultation has not taken place.

Budgetary control is an exercise in communication and if this is lacking in the first place all that follows will be at best a matter of routine checking and at worst an unheeded quarterly, monthly or weekly return. Budgetary control is much more than this. Its purpose is to involve all managers in an understanding of the financial resources under their control and to show them their contribution towards the prosperity of the enterprise.

The Budget Officer

To avoid the danger which may arise from placing this technique within the financial function, it is suggested that any business of size should have an independent budget section under a budget officer responsible directly to the managing director and whose duties would be:

(i) to involve all managers in the setting up and control of budgets; and
(ii) to involve the chief executive in all the budgetary activities.

To achieve these two objectives, the budget officer will set up the necessary meetings and discussions to establish the relevant budget. This first task would be done in full co-operation with the financial function who would possess much useful data and would certainly involve the managing director in the meeting and discussion processes. The budget officer in charge of the section would act as a link-man between the individual manager and the chief executive and it would be his duty to establish budgets which are strictly relevant to the needs of management control and which are also based on discussions with the managers concerned with their implementation.

The organization chart for a business in which budgetary control forms a separate function might appear as follows:

BOARD OF DIRECTORS
(Policy)

MANAGING
DIRECTOR
(Policy Implementation)

| SALES | BUDGET OFFICER | FINANCE | PRODUCTION |

It is stressed that the organization of budgetary control lies at the root of the success or failure of this technique. However, within any organization the need for the involvement of the chief executive is perhaps paramount. Too often delegation takes place at too early a stage and budgetary control loses much of its authority and motivation for this reason. It should be remembered that, once the policy of an enterprise has been defined by the board of directors, it is then the job of the chief executive to implement this with the assistance of the human and material resources at his disposal. In this task budgetary control is the measure which can be used, first, to set objectives for each level of management and, second, to verify their attainment or otherwise.

The participation of the chief executive in budgetary control is a key factor in its success as it will provide all those concerned with implementing the company's policies with a clear understanding of the importance he attaches to the control of financial resources.

Efficiency Levels

The setting of a budget for any activity presupposes a need to establish a level of efficiency on which the forecast will be based. In this connection efficiency might be measured along a scale from 0 to 100 and it might be decided as a policy to gauge efficiency at 60 per cent. To illustrate the use of this level in the area of material usage 100 per cent efficiency would be the least possible wastage which could occur if conditions both of price and usage were perfect. From this it would be possible to measure the 60 per cent efficiency point.

In early texts on this subject it was suggested that when budgetary control was first introduced to a business the budgets set for each area of expense and income should be based on possible attainment, but that this should be made increasingly difficult as managers became more and more accustomed to this form of control and measurement. Such texts lead the reader to believe that, when the ultimate point of management sophistication had been arrived at, all the forecasts should be set at 100 per cent efficiency level and that, although these targets could seldom be reached, such managers would be immune from normal feelings of depression and would continue to try to reduce the margin of differences between budget and actual. During recent years a study has been made of budgetary control from the point of view of behavioural scientists. From their findings it would appear that this "gradual impossibility" theory does not apply, however sophisticated managers may be. In fact, this study seems to indicate that, if you make budgets impossible to attain, managers will respond by trying not to attain the targets set at all. The study indicates that for budgetary control to work successfully there must be a chance to attain, and even to improve upon, the budgets and that the more this is possible the more managers will co-operate in the technique.

Negative and Positive Progressing

The negative response which is often found in the attitude of management towards budgetary control stems in many cases from an inclination of those who progress budgets against actual performances to ignore good and chase bad differences mercilessly. This concentration on negative variances is one which should be resisted when budgetary control is operating within an enterprise. It should always be remembered that the continuance of a good or positive difference is just as important and often far more possible than stopping a bad or negative variance. It may often be found that by concentrating upon negative differences the good ones cease to take place and, however thorough the investigations into bad variances, no way is found possible to improve the position.

It should be especially noted that budgetary control must be based on a real confidence between the reporters of the information and those to whom it is presented. For this reason the establishment of the budgets in the first place must be preceded by full discussions between those concerned with the items' progress and control. In the same way the comparison between actual and budgets must be carried out in a fair and frank manner. All differences both good and bad must be examined carefully and a constructive attitude towards such differences should be encouraged and not the attitude of a "witch hunt" that has been known to occur.

Establishing Budgets

Having decided upon the organization required for a system of budgetary control, it is now necessary to decide upon the manner of progressing budgets against actual data. To a large extent this will have been determined at the meeting which will have preceded the setting up of each budget. It should be noted that these meetings have the twofold purpose of, first, familiarizing managers with the basis on which each budget was built and, second, introducing them to each area of expense or income over which he has some measure of control.

In the discussions and meetings between those concerned with setting and those with controlling budgets, decisions will be made as to who is responsible for what income and expense. Once this has been solved, budgetary control at the base of the information pyramid is constructed around managers and to a very large extent its success will depend upon the relevance of each budget to the person for whom it is intended. The relevance of each budget cannot be overstated. Too often it is found that items are included which are not within the control of the manager for whom the budget is presented. This can have a most discouraging effect upon the person concerned when the data are progressed and adverse differences under these particular heads are shown.

Frequency of Presentation

Having decided to whom the budgets should be presented, it is now necessary to consider how frequently they should arrive in the "in" trays of the appropriate managers. It is suggested that to guide this decision two considerations should be applied:

1 How often do managers require this information? and
2 How speedily and how accurately do they require the data?

The first consideration is of very real importance as management has limited time available to inspect and act upon financial information. It is better to receive one piece of central information once a month and use it thoroughly than ignore similar data presented weekly. The frequency of budget progress returns should be discussed thoroughly with those receiving them and the need and use should be fully established.

The second point as to frequency concerns accuracy and speed. This problem has already been raised in connection with financial information presented in profit and loss statements and balance sheets. In the case of budget statements it is not only necessary to present the data accurately, but speed is also a major consideration. If action is to be taken to correct a bad or continue a good difference, speed is often vital to facilitate action. For this reason, care should be taken to determine when the actual income and expense can best be obtained. For instance, weekly-paid wages are best compared weekly, monthly-paid salaries monthly, quarterly rent quarterly, and so on.

In the case of material used in a manufacturing process, this may best be controlled when the batch of items in process have been completed or whenever the volume of material is at its lowest point, thus avoiding a large and time-consuming stock check.

In determining the frequency the convention of weekly, monthly or quarterly periods should be sacrificed wherever the speed and accuracy of presentation might be adversely affected. It should also remembered that a manager's budget for the expense under his control need not, and in most cases should not, be presented all at the same time. There is no reason why weekly wages under his control cannot be presented weekly whilst other expenses are presented monthly or quarterly or whenever else is convenient. It should always be remembered that the sooner a budget is progressed against the actual data the sooner positive corrective action can be taken.

The Manner of Presentation

It should be remembered that the more use that can be made of an original document without the necessity of transposing the information on to summary sheets such as budget progress forms, the less costly will be the presentation service. An example of the use of original documents would be passing to a manager the job cards relating to labour within his department. From these documents all the details of each man's performance can be seen, and by including the budget performance for comparison purposes the manager would have all the necessary data to study expenditure on these wages.

The use of an original document can provide speedier and less expensive information for managers as it avoids the necessity of two operations, namely transposition and checking, saving much clerical time and expense. It is suggested that anyone who is presented with financial information in the form of a budget return should make sure that, where it is summarized for his benefit, this is really necessary. It is often found that summarizing takes the form of a straight copying activity from an original document to another in the belief that managers must receive its information on a clean piece of paper. Unless management looks into such operations they will continue and the enterprise will bear the consequent costs.

Flexible or Fixed Budgets

In our discussion of budgetary control so far we have assumed a certain target level of sales around which have been built the appropriate production, administration, sales, transport, financial, cash and capital expenditure budget. A budget built up in this way is referred to as fixed, but it has serious disadvantages where the level of sales and production falls outside the set target. The reason for this stems from the fact that certain expenses are variable and some are fixed. The expenses which vary do so in relation to the level of sales or production and this means that, unless the budgets for such items are produced in relation to the actual production or sales, saving and over-spending would be shown which are unrealistic. For example, if sales were budgeted at £5,000,000 and the salesmen's commission was 2 per cent, the budgeted commission would be £100,000. If, however, sales reached £6,000,000 or £4,000,000, commission would be £120,000 or £80,000, showing an excess and saving over the fixed budget of £20,000. This is a totally irrelevant fact for management to consider and so the budget for this item should have been made flexible to take into consideration increases and decreases of sales.

Progress Returns

It is now necessary to examine the budget progress statements which might be presented for income or expense, capital expenditure and the cash flow. Each of these is illustrated in this section, together with explanations of their main features. In each case these returns should be examined in the light of the remarks made under the previous section entitled "The Manner of Presentation".

Income and Expense Budget Returns

This statement sets out actual compared with budget for the period under review and to date. The comparison with the to-date, actual, and budget column is normally considered the most relevant for management-control purposes and it is to these figures that the difference column refers. The reason for this is that it is often found that fluctuations between actual and budget, which might occur during short periods of, say, a week or a month, will right themselves, if they are of a temporary nature, in the to-date column.

It should also be noted that both value and quantity are included on the statement. It is sometimes argued that very junior managers are incapable of understanding data unless they are presented in units of quantity and that values tend to confuse such readers. This theory could be exploded by any cursory talk to such employees during pay day. However, it is suggested that quantities and volume may add to the meaning of data for every level of management when dealing with certain aspects of income or expense.

The example shows an overall budget statement for material usage in a department. It would be necessary to break this down to the different levels of management within each department. This further analysis will be found necessary in the case of most expense and income budgets.

SUGGESTED BUDGET STATEMENT FOR INCOME OR EXPENSE

Description of Income or Expense: *E.G. Material or Sales*   Month 6

Cost Centre Description	This Month		To Date			Remarks
	Actual	Budget	Actual	Budget	Difference	
Dept. A £	525	640	12,415	12,104	+311	Dept. unable to keep to budget
lbs	700	820	15,310	14,940	+370	usage in m/c shop. Investigation
						still taking place. Report due . . .
Dept. B £						
lbs						

Capital Expenditure Budget Return

This statement is prepared to review the expenditure planned and incurred on fixed assets. The comparison takes the form of a three-fold review, namely this period, to-date and total cost. The last comparison takes the actual cost to date incurred on each fixed asset investment and adds to this, if relevant, the estimate to complete the project and compares this with the total budgeted cost. This comparison provides managers with advance notice if original estimates on which the budgets have been constructed are exceeded.

It should be noted that such comparison is not applicable in cases such as the purchase of motor vehicles or plant and equipment and that in these cases the to-date column will serve the purpose perfectly adequately. However, where a long-term project is in hand, such as the extension to a factory or a new shop or store, such comparison can prove of very real help.

The total capital-expenditure budget will again be broken down into areas referring to management responsibility and the analysis will depend upon the control needs of the business.

103

Capital Project	This Month		To Date		Total Cost		Difference	Remarks
	Actual	Budget	Actual	Budget	Actual Cost plus Estimate to Complete	Total Budget Cost		
	£	£	£	£	£	£	£	
Extension to Parts Store	5,100	11,200	131,000	120,000	240,000	210,000	+30,000	Alteration to specification agreed per Directors' Minute dated ...

Cash Flow Budget Return

The cash budget is a translation of all other budgets in terms of cash. It is normal to find such budgets presented in the form of a monthly receipts-and-payments summary. From this statement it is possible to foresee whether liquid resources will be sufficient to support the policies set for the enterprise. The difference between additional profit and cash was referred to in Chapter 2 and it should be noted that a planned profit over a period of, say, twelve months ahead does not indicate that during each month of that year no overdraft will be required by the business.

The cash budget should be prepared with particular care as, if it should appear that additional cash funds will be required in any particular period, the budget statement may become a basis for overdraft or other temporary or permanent loan discussion.

A particular point to note is that this budget should be prepared taking into consideration all possible delays in the case of income and all possible anticipation in the case of expenditure. In this way, the balance shown at the end of each selected period within the budget will more likely overstate than understate the need for additional funds. This need to show the cash position in the most depressing light prevents the great danger of over-optimism which in connection with overtrading will be discussed in Chapter 6.

Budgetary Control: Conclusions

The breakdown of a main budget into various sections will follow the demands of managers. In these demands selection should be based on the principle of need and use. Very great care should be exercised by the chief executive with the budget officer to ensure that sufficient budgets are being prepared and that these are of real need and use to managers at all levels within the organization. For this

CASH BUDGET

DETAILS			MONTH																					
		1		2		3		4		...		9		10		11		12	
		Actual	Budget	Actual	Budget	Actual	Budget	Actual	Budget			Actual	Budget	Actual	Budget	Actual	Budget	Actual	Budget				
Expenditure																							
Creditors-Materials																							
Wages																							
Overheads																							
Capital Repayment																							
Fixed Asset Purchases																							
Sundries																							
TOTAL (A)																							
Income																							
Debtors																							
Cash Sales																							
Interest Received																							
Capital—Issues																							
Fixed Asset Sales																							
Sundries																							
TOTAL (B)																							
Balance b/f (C)																							
Balance c/f = (B + C) − A																							

purpose the organization of budgetary control becomes of primary importance.

Much has been written about the role of the chief executive in the supervision and organization of budgetary control, but in connection with progressing the data presented once the system is in operation his role is often described in terms of speedy delegation. It is suggested that once again the application of delegation should be tempered with an understanding of the data so dispersed.

For this reason, the chief executive should take an active part in the setting up of budgets in the first place for each function. He should also be kept fully acquainted by his function heads of the subsidiary budgets into which each main budget has been sub-divided.

It is clear that no chief executive can see all the data which are supplied within the budgetary control system. However, the very scant summaries which are sometimes seen arriving infrequently on a managing director's desk may not be all that is required. It should be especially noted that, if budgetary control as a technique is used correctly and the progressing of actual to budget data is carried out vigorously, the financial control of the business will be satisfactory and the targets set for the enterprise will be regularly reviewed. For this reason neither the managing director nor the managers can afford to delegate every aspect of this technique to their supporting managers, and the balance between delegation and immersion in detail at all levels must be finely judged.

STANDARD COSTING

The need to compare a cost of a product or service with some measure of efficiency is too strong in most cases even for the most unsophisticated manager. It has been found from experience that of the two comparative techniques—budgetary control and standard costing—the one likely to be found in one way or another in most enterprises is standard costing.

Not that the managers concerned have been able to name the technique or recognize the jargon, but a comparison of sorts has existed in the costing area. This is the beginning of standard costing. Standard costing is an addition to any costing system. This must be clearly understood, as there seems to be a mistaken belief among many managers that it is an alternative to the systems discussed in the previous chapter. This is not so. Standard costing can be applied to full or marginal costing and it can be produced where the business organizes its costing on a unit or on a process basis. It is a technique concerned with the comparison of actual cost with pre-set standards and the analysis of any differences under their various reason heads known as variances.

Evolution of Standard Costing

Standard costing is a very much evolved technique in that the step between a straight comparison of actual and forecast and the additional demand for difference analysis follows a natural demand pattern of management.

To illustrate this, we shall examine a summarized actual cost compared with a budget cost of a unit known as product A.

							PRODUCT A		
							Actual	Budget	Difference
Direct material	.	.	.	.	.	.	10	9	+1
Direct labour	.	.	.	.	.	.	8	9	−1
Expenses:									
Variable	.	.	.	.	.	.	5	6	−1
Fixed	.	.	.	.	.	.	10	9	+1
							33	33	0
							7	9	−2
Sales price	.	.	.	.	.	.	40	42	−2

From this example it will be seen that each area of expense and sales is compared with a pre-set budget and a difference is brought out. However, the purpose of such comparison is not simply to discover differences but to act so as to improve or maintain improvements in performances. For this to be achieved it is necessary to trace the reason for each difference exactly to a cause so that this can be examined and either avoided if bad or made permanent if good. In certain cases a bad difference, such as a general price increase in material, may be unavoidable. In such a case it is still necessary to isolate the cause so that it can be ignored in any steps taken at corrective action in other areas of the material difference.

Difference Analysis

DIRECT MATERIAL

The analysis of differences is necessary as many have more than one cause and are the responsibility of more than one manager. For instance, in the case of direct material in the example, the difference shown is an overspending of 1p on this item, but this is insufficient to require corrective action to be taken by management.

No indication is given as to whether this amount is caused because of a price or usage increase and in practice it could be a net difference between these two causes. Anyone concerned with cost control can tell that unless this breakdown of data is available action of an indiscriminate nature might prove very harmful. The 1p difference could be caused by a good price difference of 2p and a bad usage of 3p per product A. From a management-control viewpoint the buyer requires encouragement to see whether this purchase price cannot be repeated whilst the production manager concerned with usage needs to be asked the reason for the excess waste. There may, of course, be a connection between a lower-priced material and a high usage in that more wastage may occur with a low-priced lower-quality material and this should be investigated in the progressing stage.

DIRECT LABOUR

In the case of direct labour the 1p difference might be caused by a change in the rate of pay or by the time termed efficiency in which the production was completed. Analysis of this difference will pinpoint the managers responsible for these different causes and make possible any necessary corrective action.

EXPENSES

Before examining the reason for differences in expenses, whatever they may be, it is first necessary to divide expenses into those which are variable and those which are fixed. This is required as, in the case of an expense which is variable with either production or sales, the difference will only have one cause—a variation in the expense itself. For example, where a royalty is paid to a designer for every product produced, if a difference occurs between the budgeted royalty for product A and the actual royalty paid the reason can only be because the royalty per unit has changed, so long as the budget is constructed on the flexible basis laid down earlier in this chapter.

On the other hand, actual fixed expenses may vary from those budgeted, for many different reasons. To illustrate this point we shall examine an item for rent. The budget for this will be arrived at by first estimating the rent payable over the period in which product A will be produced. The next stage will be to arrive at a basis by which this expense can be charged to each unit as it is produced. As already explained in the chapter on costing a common basis is the direct labour hours and if this is so the budgeted fixed expenses shown will be recovered based on a budgeted number of direct labour hours going into the budgeted production of product A.

From this it will be seen that, if the difference of 1p between actual and budgeted fixed expenses in product A refers to rent, it may be caused by a change in the actual rent paid from budget, i.e. an expense difference. It could also be caused if the actual direct labour hours differ from those budgeted in the production of product A. A difference of this nature may have more than one cause. For example, if direct labour does not perform the task of producing product A within the stipulated time, this may be due to the fact that they did or did not work hard enough, or that they were delayed because of a lack of materials or for countless other reasons.

Each of these reasons may be significant to management in their control of the enterprise as it will highlight the cost of not achieving the direct labour hours on which fixed expense recovery is based. Thinking back into marginal costing it should be remembered that the cost of any delay in output is the cost of fixed expenses which will continue during this period.

It should be noted that the use of the example of product A in connection with the analysis of fixed-expense variance is for illustration purposes and that actual fixed expenses will be determined at period and not product or service end. Thus, in the case of product A, if the fixed expense budget rate is 50p per direct labour hour, the budgeted time is fixed at 0·9 hours, whilst it has actually taken 1·0 hour. The 50p rate will be verified at period end and the breakdown of the 0·1 hour difference is all that can be achieved in practice at this stage of the examination.

SALES

The difference between actual and budgeted sales price relates in the case of one product such as A to a price change. However, if the actual sales prices of all products are compared in total with those of the budget for a period the difference revealed might have more than one cause.

First, there may have been an alteration in the price per unit. Second, the actual sales might be as great as, less or greater than the budget in volume. Third, if different products make up the budget the budget will be based on a particular mix which if not achieved might be a further cause of the difference. We shall now examine an illustration setting out these three types of difference.

From this illustration it will be seen that the budgeted sales for the period are based on a given volume of sales in a set mix at the budgeted and standard price per unit. The actual sales are then shown and the total difference shown is £210, which is unfavourable.

The standard sales are then set out, which are the actual sales in total expressed in the budgeted mix and at the standard price per

	Budgeted Sales					Actual Sales	
	Units	%		£			£
A	1,000	25	× 50p =	500	A	400 × 50p =	200
B	500	12½	× 40p =	200	B	700 × 30p =	210
C	500	12½	× 35p =	175	C	300 × 45p =	135
D	2,000	50	× 30p =	600	D	1,800 × 40p =	720
	4,000	100		£1,475		3,200	£1,265

Total Differences (£1,475 − £1,265) = £210 adverse

	Standard Sales					Actual Sales at Standard Price	
	Units	%		£			£
A	800	25	× 50p =	400	A	400 × 50p =	200
B	400	12½	× 40p =	160	B	700 × 40p =	280
C	400	12½	× 35p =	140	C	300 × 35p =	105
D	1,600	50	× 30p =	480	D	1,800 × 30p =	540
	3,200	100		£1,180			£1,125

	£
Price Variance (£1,265 − £1,125) =	140 favourable
Mix Variance (£1,125 − £1,180) =	− 55 adverse
Volume Variance (£1,180 − £1,475) =	−295 adverse
Net Difference	£210 adverse

unit. The actual sales in the actual mix and calculated at the standard price per unit are compared with the actual value of the actual sales, to show the price variance of £140, which is favourable. The actual sales in the actual mix at the standard price per unit are compared with the standard sales and the difference of £55 unfavourable relates to the mix variance. The last difference, which refers to the fall in volume of sales, is calculated by taking the standard sales from the budgeted sales and this gives an unfavourable variance of £295. The net of these three differences adds up to a net unfavourable difference of £210.

Preliminary

(a) SETTING STANDARDS
Standard costing is therefore designed to assist managers in determining exactly where differences have occurred. It is a system for isolating reasons and determining causes and it starts in the same way as budgetary control, by the setting up of comparisons. These comparisons are termed standards, but they are no different from

any other form of forecast, target or budget. They are estimates as to what will happen in the particular areas of expense and income. However, it is normal to find that a business which installs a system of standard costing goes to some trouble to establish the standards concerned.

Many consultants would believe that to introduce this system of comparison it would first be necessary to establish trustworthy standards for both material and labour and would feel that there was a prerequisite for material control with wastage standards and work study with time standards before proceeding with a standard costing installation. The reason for this is that standard costing takes comparison to its ultimate conclusion in the costing area. If so much analysis and comparison is to take place with the relating administration costs, the facts presented should be based upon the best possible data which can be made available. For this reason, to guess a time for labour, or to select from past records the material content of a particular process, would be an inadequate framework around which to build this complex comparative system.

Standards are, therefore, normally based on the best possible data which can be made available and where there is a lack of data, this must be remedied before proceeding to the refinement of standard costing comparison.

(*b*) VOLUME OF DATA

The analysis required in standard costing is so extensive that the system should be installed only where there is a real need coupled with a real intention to use the data provided. If properly installed and controlled, however, the system will lead through management by objectives into management by exception in that each failure to reach pre-set targets will be investigated and the reason disclosed, thus concentrating managers' attention to the exception areas.

It is so important that all managers should understand the volume of work entailed in setting up a standard costing system that we give below an example of the way a standard for an element of cost is assembled, showing how, as the actual costs are incurred, they are analysed in a similar way and the appropriate variances are computed.

When we consider that, for each element of expense, standards and actuals will be required for each stage of production and these will need to be calculated, the volume of work may be appreciated. In a similar manner analysis will be required for both variable and fixed expense. It should be noted that, apart from the problem of arriving at the standards and the analysis of the actual data, each variance involves an arithmetic calculation.

111

Standard Calculation = Standard Time × Standard Rate of Pay per hour
Actual Calculation = Actual Time × Actual Rate of Pay per hour

Example: Standard Time = 8 hours
Standard Rate = 75p per hour

Actual Time = 9 hours
Actual Rate = 80p per hour

Total Difference = (8 × 75p) − (9 × 80p) = £1·20 bad

Rate Variance = 9 hrs (80p − 75p) = 0·45 bad
Efficiency Variance = 75p (9 − 8) = 0·75 bad

£1·20 total

MANAGEMENT DEMANDS AND NEEDS

Standard costing is therefore a system that must be an answer to a real need and the involvement of all management concerned is a prerequisite of its provision. Many enterprises adopt a limited system of standard costing and apply this technique to the control of only certain expenses whilst leaving the others under the control of the budgetary control system.

In such cases it is normal to find the direct and variable expenses and sales income controlled by standard costing and fixed expenses left to be controlled by budgets. By not applying standard costing to fixed expenses the cost of not fulfilling the recovery basis, outlined in a previous paragraph, will not be measured in terms of under- or over-recovered fixed expenses.

The difference for each item of expense and income will be analysed under their separate causes as explained in the previous paragraph and these are known as variances. The expense of installing and running a standard costing system will be determined by two factors:

(i) the number of standards required to establish the system; and
(ii) the volume of variance analysis required.

In the case of the first factor, it should be noted that the standards set for standard costing should have uses outside this technique. Thus, material and labour controls are necessary for production control and in fact their use within a system of standard costing is more a by-product of their provision than their main use.

This should be made true wherever possible, of all standards set for this system. In each case the standards set should have more than one use and the standard costing use should not be the major one.

The second factor, the volume of variance analysis required, must be determined by the needs of managers. It is essential that the provision of this financial technique should be accompanied by real management interest. This interest should be of an active variety and include discussion and understanding at every stage of its installation. The provision of too many or too few variances can greatly damage the effectiveness of the technique as well as having a considerable effect under the administration cost.

COMPARISON FREQUENCY

In this connection care should be taken in deciding when actual cost data should be compared with the standards set. This has been mentioned in connection with budgetary control but it is equally important to establish for standard costing. In this case it is vital to analyse differences as and when they occur and not necessarily to await normal reporting dates such as week, month or quarter ends. For example, material price variance should be reported as soon as materials are purchased and prices known. However, material usage variances will be presented as and when they occur and are known during the production processes.

In the case of labour, the rate variance will be reported when and if it occurs and the efficiency of labour to work within the standard time set will be presented when the facts are known, which will in many cases be at weekends from data contained in the job cards and time sheets.

The reporting of variances should as often as possible be included with other information relating to the same item of expense or income. For example, variance of fixed expense should be included in the relevant budgetary-control progress statement for the particular type and area of expense.

INTRODUCTION BY STAGES

The complexity and volume of data stemming from a standard costing system can create very high administrative costs and it is suggested that much of this material can be avoided if the implementation of this system is done in stages and no barrier is created between one information system and another.

For example, if standard costing is to be introduced, the first step is to select the element of cost or sales to which the system will first be applied. If we assume that we select direct labour it is first necessary to assemble all the data at present available on this item. From this the amount of data presented to management can be seen and wherever possible any additional presentation necessitated by introducing standard costing should either be combined with or replace existing data.

It is always useful to take a section of the selected expenses or income and deal with this in some detail. This enables management to see what information can be presented and to experiment with different methods of presentation to find out which is more suitable to management needs. This approach to introducing standard costing can be of great assistance in reducing the cost of administering the system and also in bringing its relevance to the notice of all managers concerned.

Conclusion

It is suggested that unless there is a real demand for this system of cost control and comparison it is best not introduced to the business, as the cost will not be compensated by the resultant advantages. It is vital that all managers understand the system thoroughly and in this connection their ability to question the need for particular variances and to request additional ones should be inherent within any system.

5   *Investment of Capital*

The balance sheet tells you from where the business obtained its capital and where it is invested. It can be described as a statement showing the source and application of the wealth of the enterprise. In this chapter we shall concentrate upon the application of capital and we shall therefore be concerned with investment within a business.

THE INVESTMENT DECISION

Every business has three areas in which it can invest its capital. These are:

    (i) fixed assets;
    (ii) working capital; and
    (iii) investments outside the enterprise.

The investment in a business takes the form of a three-part portfolio and wherever and whenever there is capital to invest managers must decide how much should go into each area. In fact, however, capital often goes into one category or another without any preliminary management decision. This may be because the enterprise is run in an undisciplined manner or it may be because capital is urgently needed in one area and no special decision is necessary. An example of this type of investment is the purchase of safety equipment following a report by a factory inspector.

In the first chapter the financial objective of business was set out as maximizing return on capital employed. In order to achieve this aim, the foundation must be prepared by making the right investments in the first place. In the same way as an investor in shares depends upon how his capital has been invested for his return in the form of dividends, so the profit or loss of an enterprise will be determined by the underlying investment. The main areas of investment must fulfil two objectives: first, the purchase of the right fixed assets and second, the adequacy of the amount invested in working capital.

It must always be remembered that, as in other investment fields, a mistake now will influence returns and profits for many years ahead. This is especially true of investment of the long-term variety, i.e. fixed assets, but certain working-capital investment such as stocks may also call for the locking up of money for a considerable period of time.

INVESTMENT SELECTION

The understanding that the real strength of a company depends upon where the capital is invested has led the thoughtful manager to seek answers to two questions. In the first place, to find out whether or not the business should invest in specific fixed assets a series of what are known as investment-appraisal techniques have been produced to assist the manager. They consist of measures against the cost of the proposed fixed-assets investment and these are discussed in detail in the following section.

The second question is whether or not the capital invested in working capital is adequate or not, but this cannot be answered by the use of a measure against investment as in the case of fixed assets. The control of working capital is without doubt a difficult matter but it will nevertheless form the spring-board for the expansion of any enterprise.

The objective of management in this area is to make no investment at all, or at least to minimize it as far as possible. If this can be achieved, it will mean that all capital invested in the business will be made in fixed assets and outside investments. Because there is no need for working capital, expansion of the business will be limited only by either a lack of fixed assets, e.g. factory capacity or shelf-space limits, or the saleability of its products or services. To achieve this position working capital must be examined carefully and each investment area within working capital such as stock, debtors, etc., analysed to see whether it is being kept at its minimum. The technique of working-capital analysis will be dealt with in detail later in this chapter.

Investment outside the business will be made by management based on their assessment of the individual situation and as explained previously may be motivated by more than one reason. These may include the ability to improve the return on the capital investment for such funds if they are diverted into outside investments. Again such investment may take place in order to take over, that is obtain control of, another enterprise by purchasing more than half of its voting shares and thus controlling its board of directors. The methods used to justify investment outside a business will vary and will range from an assessment of future dividends and capital security to a full-scale financial trading investigation which would precede a takeover bid.

Fixed Assets

If the management can successfully limit investment in working capital to nil and no outside investments are made, all the capital invested in the enterprise will be in fixed assets. From this it will be seen that any return investors are seeking in the business will have to be associated with the investment in fixed assets.

This can be illustrated as follows:

X LTD

BALANCE SHEET

As at 31 December 19. .

			£
FIXED ASSETS			150,000
WORKING CAPITAL			
Current Assets:			
Stocks	£60,000		
Debtors	120,000		
Cash	2,000		
		£182,000	
Less: Current Liabilities:			
Creditors		182,000	—
			150,000
SHARE CAPITAL			100,000
RESERVES			30,000
DEBENTURES			20,000
			£150,000

If, in the above-mentioned company, the shareholders look for a return of 15 per cent, it is vital that when each investment in fixed assets is made, management is assured that it will provide a return of at least this amount.

However, fixed assets are unlike most other forms of investment in that, as well as being required to provide a reasonable return, they must in many cases also provide funds for their own replacement. That is to say that, with the exception of freehold land, they are subject to a limited life span. This limit is caused by the fact that the value of many fixed assets will have disappeared either through wear and tear as in the case of buildings and plant and machinery, etc., or by the expiry of time as in the case of leasehold property. A further cause for the loss in value of fixed assets is obsolescence and this is an increasingly prominent factor in the case of such items as plant and machinery in the advanced technological industries.

FIXED-ASSET BUDGETS

As previously explained, fixed assets are the foundation of future profits and determine the trading activities of the business for the years ahead. For this reason, before applying any appraisal techniques it is first necessary to establish a clear system of fixed-assets (often termed "capital-expenditure") budgeting. This technique was explained in Chapter 4 and such a budget must be prepared for the enterprise irrespective of what techniques are used to appraise each particular fixed-asset investment proposal.

The budget will set out the areas and the proposed amount of investment for each area of fixed assets over the years ahead, and this will be agreed in total by the top management of the organization. This overall budget will be prepared in considerable detail and will be based on the best possible data available at the time of its preparation. It is normal for the top management to delegate the administration of the capital-expenditure budget to a sub-committee which would be concerned with two matters:

(i) to link up each fixed-asset investment proposed during the future years with the agreed budget; and

(ii) to assess whether or not the particular investment fulfils the criteria set by the organization.

These two stages must be recognized and steps taken to ensure compliance with them. When a fixed asset is proposed it is first necessary to check with the budget to see that the proposal is in order from an overall investment point of view and, second, to check that it comes up to the measures laid down for the investment. The first point has already been discussed under "Budgets" in Chapter 4 and it is now necessary to examine the criteria used to measure individual investment.

NET CASH FLOW

The techniques which have become available for managers to assess fixed-assets investments have to some extent evolved over the years, but in each case they have been built up to solve one or both of the problems of finding out the adequacy of the return and of providing funds to replace the original investment. For this reason, they each use the same measure—the net cash flow related to the cost of the capital investment, i.e. the fixed asset.

It is found that whenever a technique is used to assess fixed-asset investment two pieces of information will be required. First, the cost of the fixed asset proposed and, second, the net cash flow which it is believed will arise because of the investment. The concept of net cash flow is not one which comes easily to accountants who are used to measuring returns in terms of net profit or loss. However, this latter measure is incorrect in the case of fixed-assets appraisal as net profit attributed to a particular fixed asset would bring into account two factors which would obscure the assessment, viz. that net profit or loss is:

(i) subject to depreciation; and
(ii) is arrived at in the case of a fixed asset among other fixed assets after the reallocation of overhead and such reallocation would be irrelevant in the assessment.

The first point regarding depreciation is important as each technique used to assess depreciating fixed assets measures not just the return on the investment but also the recovery of the investment out of funds flowing into the business because of the investment. Thus, suppose that A Ltd invested £40,000 in plant and machinery in year 0 and the net cash flow forecast over the next five years, which is the anticipated life of the item, is as follows:

Year	£
1	8,000
2	12,000
3	12,000
4	10,000
5	6,000

Any assessment of this item would consider in the first place whether the net cash flows are sufficient to replace the cost of the investment. This is based on the assumption that at the end of five years the investment has no value or that if it has scrap value it is included in the £6,000 recorded in the net cash flow for year 5. For this reason it would be incorrect to deduct depreciation before striking the net cash flow figure each year as this would mean assessing the original investment twice.

119

The problem of the reallocation of overheads is best illustrated from an example such as the one set out below:

A new machine Y is to be installed which will have an additional output and will increase sales by £30,000. The additional material and labour cost for these units will be £20,000 and £6,000 respectively, and depreciation on the new machine will be £7,000 per annum. The departmental costs before and after the instalment are as follows:

	Before £	After £
Rent	3,000	3,000
Rates	300	300
Insurance . . .	1,200	1,260
Foreman's salary . . .	1,100	1,200
Indirect labour . . .	2,000	2,400

The calculation of the net profit or loss and net cash flow for machine Y is as follows:

NET PROFIT OR LOSS CALCULATION

		£
Additional Sales		30,000
	£	
Less: Material	20,000	
Labour	6,000	
Rent ($\frac{1}{6}$ × £3,000)	500	
Rates ($\frac{1}{6}$ × £300)	50	
Insurance ($\frac{1}{6}$ × £1,260)	210	
Foreman's salary ($\frac{1}{6}$ × £1,200) . .	200	
Indirect wages ($\frac{1}{6}$ × £2,400) . . .	400	
Depreciation	7,000	
		34,360
Net Loss		£4,360

NET CASH FLOW CALCULATION

		£
Additional Sales		30,000
	£	
Less: Material	20,000	
Labour	6,000	
Rent	—	
Rates	—	
Insurance (£1,200–£1,260) . . .	60	
Foreman's salary (£1,100–£1,200) . .	100	
Indirect labour (£2,000–£2,400) . .	400	
Depreciation	—	
		26,560
Gross Cash Flow *		£3,440 (Positive)

* After taxation, becomes the Net Cash Flow (N.C.F.).

120

The measure of net cash flow can be likened to the additional cash which will flow into your pocket if you take certain action as opposed to not taking it. It ignores depreciation as the measure is solely concerned with cash items—both expenses and income—and is therefore unconcerned with this type of adjustment entry. It is also only concerned with additional expenses which arise because of the particular investment and not with any reapportionment of expenses such as takes place in a profit and loss calculation.

It is important that this measure and the difference between it and the computation of the net profit or loss should be clearly understood by management. This is because it may not be familiar to all accountants as it stems from the theory of economists, and for this reason accountants may incorrectly select net profit or loss as the measure and this may produce very different results from those shown from the net cash flow as in the previous illustration.

ASSESSMENT MEASURE AND ADJUSTMENTS

The net cash flow should also include the effect of taxation on the business because of the particular fixed-asset investment. This will include corporation tax on any increased profits and capital allowances relating to the fixed-asset purchase. To become familiar with these two tax adjustments readers should approach their company accountants to outline the principle of taxation in this area.

The data required for assessing fixed assets will be common for whichever technique is used by the enterprise. In setting up a system of fixed-asset appraisal it is vital that all managers concerned with presenting requests for such investments are fully aware how such data can be prepared and presented. It is the task of the manager proposing the investment to obtain the data and this task should not be delegated entirely to the financial function. The reason for this is to make sure that all concerned are involved in the appraisal technique and are fully aware of whether or not their proposals measure up to the criteria set. It may be found that part of the net cash flow computation such as taxation is beyond the capability of the non-financial managers.

This should not preclude understanding and in these cases it is suggested that as much data as possible should be prepared by the manager proposing the investment and passed to the financial function for completion. Care should be taken by such managers to obtain a full explanation of any additional data inserted at this point so that they can be understood.

121

9

Having examined the measure used to assess fixed-asset investment we shall now examine the appraisal methods which are:

  (i) pay-back;
  (ii) interest on capital investment;
  (iii) discounted cash flow.

These methods have been developed to meet this particular management need and are discussed below under their individual heads.

Pay-back Method

The pay-back method is perhaps the earliest technique used in this area of investment. It is certainly true that some years ago a survey of investment-appraisal techniques used in the midlands showed this method to be the one most favoured by local industry. As a method it confines its concern to measuring the time in which the investment cost will be recovered from the net cash flow which arises following the fixed-asset investment. It therefore concentrates its attention upon the factor of obsolescence and has a very real application in a fast-changing technological age.

To illustrate this method, let us consider the following data presented by a manager wishing to purchase a particular piece of machinery:

Estimated cost of machinery   £30,000

Year	Net Cash Flow £
1	5,000
2	10,000
3	15,000
4	8,000
5	2,000

Applying the pay-back method of assessment to this information one finds that in three years the accumulated net cash flow will be sufficient to equal the capital cost of £30,000 (£5,000 plus £10,000 plus £15,000). This is referred to as a three-year pay-back and under this method agreement to invest will depend upon whether or not this period of return of capital is considered satisfactory. The importance of recognizing the need to reimburse a business for the capital invested in its fixed assets is such that this method holds out considerable attraction to many enterprises. Even where other appraisal methods are used the pay-back method is often combined with these.

Average Interest on Capital Invested

This second method is set out here to show the evolution of the appraisal techniques rather than as a method in current use by business. In fact, it is some ten years since I last saw it in practice, but it nevertheless illustrates the development of the idea of return on capital employed. It is suggested that if anyone who had little knowledge of finance were asked to invent an appraisal technique, it is likely that he would come back with this method. It expresses very simply the measure of return on capital invested and its application is illustrated below from the data used in the previous example for the pay-back method.

		£
Cost of proposed fixed-asset investment		30,000

Year	Net Cash Flow
1	£5,000
2	10,000
3	15,000
4	8,000
5	2,000

Total	40,000
Less	30,000 = Original cost of investment

$$10,000 \div 5 = £2,000 = 13 \cdot 3\% \text{ on } \frac{£30,000}{2}$$

The net cash flow is totalled over the five years and from this is subtracted the investment cost of £30,000. The difference of £10,000 represents the surplus net cash flow and the average over each of the five years is £2,000. This amount is then expressed as a percentage return on the average capital invested. It is assumed that the £30,000 is written off equally each year from 0 to 5 years and the average is thus calculated as £30,000 ÷ 2 = £15,000

As stated above, this method is the one which is perhaps the most logical to understand by the layman, but it suffers from one very real disadvantage. It ignores the fact that, when someone is considering an investment in the light of the return which will be obtained from it, the return should be calculated as compound and not simple interest. The interest of 13·3 per cent calculated above is simple and not compound, and as such is an unsatisfactory measure for anyone considering the adequacy of the return over any length of time.

Discounted Cash Flow Method

The third method which has developed enormously over recent years goes under the rather confusing title of discounted cash flow (abbreviated as D.C.F.). As a method it is concerned with return on capital invested as is the previous technique, but unlike the previous method it takes into consideration compound and not simple interest. It is based on the belief that a bird in the hand is worth two in the bush which in financial terms can be related to the fact that a net cash flow received in year 1 of £5,000 is worth more than a N.C.F. of £5,000 received in years 2, 3, 4, etc. The reason for this is that the sooner the cash is received the sooner it can be put to use and therefore the £5,000 received in year 1 will be worth at least £5,000 plus compound interest at the lowest possible rate in years 2, 3, 4, etc.

Once this fact about finance is understood, it is possible to approach fixed-asset appraisal in this manner. The N.C.F. which is calculated for each of the years in which the particular fixed asset will be used by any enterprise must fulfil two objectives:

(i) replace the original investment cash, which will be necessary in all cases except freehold land; and

(ii) provide a reasonable return on the capital invested.

To answer these two points there is available a series of discount tables constructed to show how much requires to be invested now at whatever rate of compound interest is selected which will amount to one unit of currency in any number of years ahead. The tables have been available for centuries to finance houses, but in recent years they have been found to have an application in assessing the real worth of future profits or net cash flows.

By applying the appropriate factor for a particular rate of interest it is possible to determine in a fixed-asset decision whether or not the net cash flows equal a return at the particular interest rate and also reimburse the business with the original cost of the investment to the business. To illustrate this method of fixed-asset appraisal, we shall examine the data presented in the previous illustration and apply the factor relating to the return sought by this business, namely 10 per cent after taxation. The discount factors for this interest rate are found from table A on page 126.

The application of the D.C.F. investment-appraisal technique is set out on page 125.

It will be seen from this example that the effect of applying the discount factor to each cash flow for each year is to strip the compound interest content from each amount and to leave the sum termed the present value, which is the amount which, if invested in year 0 at 10 per cent compound interest, would produce the particular net cash flow in the respective years. The discount factor is therefore a conversion factor to determine how much is required

Year
0   Fixed Asset Investment Cash—Proposed £30,000

	N.C.F.		D.F.		Present Value
	£				£
1	5,000	×	0·909	=	4,545
2	10,000	×	0·826	=	8,260
3	15,000	×	0·751	=	11,265
4	8,000	×	0·683	=	5,464
5	2,000	×	0·621	=	1,242
					30,776

to be invested now at whatever rate of compound interest is selected to produce the sum forecast to be received in x number of years. Hence it has a very real application in the area of fixed assets for, if the product of the present values equals or exceeds the original sum invested, as in the illustration, it will prove that the net cash flow equals the criteria rate of return and also provides a reimbursement to the enterprise of the original investment cost.

Tables such as those on pages 126 and 127 are available for rates of interest from 0 to 100 per cent and for any year hence. They are also available to show net cash flows which will be received in whichever way is applicable, e.g. to take into consideration a seasonal pattern of receipts and payments.

Interest Rate Selection

The selected rate of interest will depend upon the particular enterprise but it will be determined by the top management, who are responsible for ensuring a satisfactory return on the capital employed. It is advisable to use more than one rate of interest as it would be unreasonable to expect every fixed asset to provide the same return. For instance, the return on some items of research equipment might be very small as compared with that on a piece of manufacturing machinery. However, it may nevertheless be essential for investment to be made in this area. To meet this situation management using this method must lay down a series of interest rates applicable to different classes of fixed assets. This selection of rates presupposes an overall capital-expenditure budget which will allow for this disparity of rates knowing that the total expenditure on fixed assets must make possible an adequate investment return.

The determination of present values in total equal to the original capital investment applies only to fixed assets which after a period of time are worth nothing except their scrap value which will be

DISCOUNT TABLE

Table A: Present Value of £1 Received Annually

Years Hence	1%	2%	4%	6%	8%	10%	12%	14%	15%	16%	18%	20%	22%	24%	25%	26%	28%	30%	35%	40%	45%	50%
1	0·990	0·980	0·962	0·943	0·926	0·909	0·893	0·877	0·870	0·862	0·847	0·833	0·820	0·806	0·800	0·794	0·781	0·769	0·741	0·714	0·690	0·667
2	0·980	0·961	0·925	0·890	0·857	0·826	0·797	0·769	0·756	0·743	0·718	0·694	0·672	0·650	0·640	0·630	0·610	0·592	0·549	0·510	0·476	0·444
3	0·971	0·942	0·889	0·840	0·794	0·751	0·712	0·675	0·658	0·641	0·609	0·579	0·551	0·524	0·512	0·500	0·477	0·455	0·406	0·364	0·328	0·296
4	0·961	0·924	0·855	0·792	0·735	0·683	0·636	0·592	0·572	0·552	0·516	0·482	0·451	0·423	0·410	0·397	0·373	0·350	0·301	0·260	0·226	0·198
5	0·951	0·906	0·822	0·747	0·681	0·621	0·567	0·519	0·497	0·476	0·437	0·402	0·370	0·341	0·328	0·315	0·291	0·269	0·223	0·186	0·156	0·132
6	0·942	0·888	0·790	0·705	0·630	0·564	0·507	0·456	0·432	0·410	0·370	0·335	0·303	0·275	0·262	0·250	0·227	0·207	0·165	0·133	0·108	0·088
7	0·933	0·871	0·760	0·665	0·583	0·513	0·452	0·400	0·376	0·354	0·314	0·279	0·249	0·222	0·210	0·198	0·178	0·159	0·122	0·095	0·074	0·059
8	0·923	0·853	0·731	0·627	0·540	0·467	0·404	0·351	0·327	0·305	0·266	0·233	0·204	0·179	0·168	0·157	0·139	0·123	0·091	0·068	0·051	0·039
9	0·914	0·837	0·703	0·592	0·500	0·424	0·361	0·308	0·284	0·263	0·225	0·194	0·167	0·144	0·134	0·125	0·108	0·094	0·067	0·048	0·035	0·026
10	0·905	0·820	0·676	0·558	0·463	0·386	0·322	0·270	0·247	0·227	0·191	0·162	0·137	0·116	0·107	0·099	0·085	0·073	0·050	0·035	0·024	0·017
11	0·896	0·804	0·650	0·527	0·429	0·350	0·287	0·237	0·215	0·195	0·162	0·135	0·112	0·094	0·086	0·079	0·066	0·056	0·037	0·025	0·017	0·012
12	0·887	0·788	0·625	0·497	0·397	0·319	0·257	0·208	0·187	0·168	0·137	0·112	0·092	0·076	0·069	0·062	0·052	0·043	0·027	0·018	0·012	0·008
13	0·879	0·773	0·601	0·469	0·368	0·290	0·229	0·182	0·163	0·145	0·116	0·093	0·075	0·061	0·055	0·050	0·040	0·033	0·020	0·013	0·008	0·005
14	0·870	0·758	0·577	0·442	0·340	0·263	0·205	0·160	0·141	0·125	0·099	0·078	0·062	0·049	0·044	0·039	0·032	0·025	0·015	0·009	0·006	0·003
15	0·861	0·743	0·555	0·417	0·315	0·239	0·183	0·140	0·123	0·108	0·084	0·065	0·051	0·040	0·035	0·031	0·025	0·020	0·011	0·006	0·004	0·002
16	0·853	0·728	0·534	0·394	0·292	0·218	0·163	0·123	0·107	0·093	0·071	0·054	0·042	0·032	0·028	0·025	0·019	0·015	0·008	0·005	0·003	0·002
17	0·844	0·714	0·513	0·371	0·270	0·198	0·146	0·108	0·093	0·080	0·060	0·045	0·034	0·026	0·023	0·020	0·015	0·012	0·006	0·003	0·002	0·001
18	0·836	0·700	0·494	0·350	0·250	0·180	0·130	0·095	0·081	0·069	0·051	0·038	0·028	0·021	0·018	0·016	0·012	0·009	0·005	0·002	0·001	0·001
19	0·828	0·686	0·475	0·331	0·232	0·164	0·116	0·083	0·070	0·060	0·043	0·031	0·023	0·017	0·014	0·012	0·009	0·007	0·003	0·002	0·001	
20	0·820	0·673	0·456	0·312	0·215	0·149	0·104	0·073	0·061	0·051	0·037	0·026	0·019	0·014	0·012	0·010	0·007	0·005	0·002	0·001	0·001	
21	0·811	0·660	0·439	0·294	0·199	0·135	0·093	0·064	0·053	0·044	0·031	0·022	0·015	0·011	0·009	0·008	0·006	0·004	0·002	0·001		
22	0·803	0·647	0·422	0·278	0·184	0·123	0·083	0·056	0·046	0·038	0·026	0·018	0·013	0·009	0·007	0·006	0·004	0·003	0·001	0·001		
23	0·795	0·634	0·406	0·262	0·170	0·112	0·074	0·049	0·040	0·033	0·022	0·015	0·010	0·007	0·006	0·005	0·003	0·002	0·001			
24	0·788	0·622	0·390	0·247	0·158	0·102	0·066	0·043	0·035	0·028	0·019	0·013	0·008	0·007	0·005	0·004	0·003	0·002	0·001			
25	0·780	0·610	0·375	0·233	0·146	0·092	0·059	0·038	0·030	0·024	0·016	0·010	0·007	0·006	0·004	0·003	0·002	0·001	0·001			
26	0·772	0·598	0·361	0·220	0·135	0·084	0·053	0·033	0·026	0·021	0·014	0·009	0·006	0·005	0·003	0·002	0·002	0·001				
27	0·764	0·586	0·347	0·207	0·125	0·076	0·047	0·029	0·023	0·018	0·011	0·007	0·005	0·004	0·002	0·002	0·001	0·001				
28	0·757	0·574	0·333	0·196	0·116	0·069	0·042	0·026	0·020	0·016	0·010	0·006	0·004	0·003	0·002	0·001	0·001	0·001				
29	0·749	0·563	0·321	0·185	0·107	0·063	0·037	0·022	0·017	0·014	0·008	0·005	0·003	0·002	0·002	0·001	0·001	0·001				
30	0·742	0·552	0·308	0·174	0·099	0·057	0·033	0·020	0·015	0·012	0·007	0·004	0·003	0·002	0·001	0·001	0·001	0·001				
40	0·672	0·453	0·208	0·097	0·046	0·022	0·011	0·005	0·004	0·003	0·001	0·001										
50	0·608	0·372	0·141	0·054	0·021	0·009	0·003	0·001	0·001	0·001												

Table B: Present Value of £1 Received Annually for N Years

Years Hence	1%	2%	4%	6%	8%	10%	12%	14%	15%	16%	18%	20%	22%	24%	25%	26%	28%	30%	35%	40%	45%	50%
1	0·990	0·980	0·962	0·943	0·926	0·909	0·893	0·877	0·870	0·862	0·847	0·833	0·820	0·806	0·800	0·794	0·781	0·769	0·741	0·714	0·690	0·667
2	1·970	1·942	1·886	1·833	1·783	1·736	1·690	1·647	1·626	1·605	1·566	1·528	1·492	1·457	1·440	1·424	1·392	1·361	1·289	1·224	1·165	1·111
3	2·941	2·884	2·775	2·673	2·577	2·487	2·402	2·322	2·283	2·246	2·174	2·106	2·042	1·981	1·952	1·923	1·868	1·816	1·696	1·589	1·493	1·407
4	3·902	3·808	3·630	3·465	3·312	3·170	3·037	2·914	2·855	2·798	2·690	2·589	2·494	2·404	2·362	2·320	2·241	2·166	1·997	1·849	1·720	1·605
5	4·853	4·713	4·452	4·212	3·993	3·791	3·605	3·433	3·352	3·274	3·127	2·991	2·864	2·745	2·689	2·635	2·532	2·436	2·220	2·035	1·876	1·737
6	5·795	5·601	5·242	4·917	4·623	4·355	4·111	3·889	3·784	3·685	3·498	3·326	3·167	3·020	2·951	2·885	2·759	2·643	2·385	2·168	1·983	1·824
7	6·728	6·472	6·002	5·582	5·206	4·868	4·564	4·288	4·160	4·039	3·812	3·605	3·416	3·242	3·161	3·083	2·937	2·802	2·508	2·263	2·057	1·883
8	7·652	7·325	6·733	6·210	5·747	5·335	4·968	4·639	4·487	4·344	4·078	3·837	3·619	3·421	3·329	3·241	3·076	2·925	2·598	2·331	2·108	1·922
9	8·566	8·162	7·435	6·802	6·247	5·759	5·328	4·946	4·772	4·607	4·303	4·031	3·786	3·566	3·463	3·366	3·184	3·019	2·665	2·379	2·144	1·948
10	9·471	8·983	8·111	7·360	6·710	6·145	5·650	5·216	5·019	4·833	4·494	4·192	3·923	3·682	3·571	3·465	3·269	3·092	2·715	2·414	2·168	1·965
11	10·368	9·787	8·760	7·887	7·139	6·495	5·988	5·453	5·234	5·029	4·656	4·327	4·035	3·776	3·656	3·544	3·335	3·147	2·752	2·438	2·185	1·977
12	11·255	10·575	9·385	8·384	7·536	6·814	6·194	5·660	5·421	5·197	4·793	4·439	4·127	3·851	3·725	3·606	3·387	3·190	2·779	2·456	2·196	1·985
13	12·134	11·343	9·986	8·853	7·904	7·103	6·424	5·842	5·583	5·342	4·910	4·533	4·203	3·912	3·780	3·656	3·427	3·223	2·799	2·468	2·204	1·990
14	13·004	12·106	10·563	9·295	8·244	7·367	6·628	6·002	5·724	5·468	5·008	4·611	4·265	3·962	3·824	3·695	3·459	3·249	2·814	2·477	2·210	1·993
15	13·865	12·849	11·118	9·712	8·559	7·606	6·811	6·142	5·847	5·575	5·092	4·675	4·315	4·001	3·859	3·726	3·483	3·268	2·825	2·484	2·214	1·995
16	14·718	13·578	11·652	10·106	8·851	7·824	6·974	6·265	5·954	5·669	5·162	4·730	4·357	4·033	3·887	3·751	3·503	3·283	2·834	2·489	2·216	1·997
17	15·562	14·292	12·166	10·477	9·122	8·022	7·120	6·373	6·047	5·749	5·222	4·775	4·391	4·059	3·910	3·771	3·518	3·295	2·840	2·492	2·218	1·998
18	16·398	14·992	12·659	10·828	9·372	8·201	7·250	6·467	6·128	5·818	5·273	4·812	4·419	4·080	3·928	3·786	3·529	3·304	2·844	2·494	2·219	1·999
19	17·226	15·678	13·134	11·158	9·604	8·365	7·366	6·550	6·198	5·877	5·316	4·844	4·442	4·097	3·942	3·799	3·539	3·311	2·848	2·496	2·220	1·999
20	18·046	16·351	13·590	11·470	9·818	8·514	7·469	6·623	6·259	5·929	5·353	4·870	4·460	4·110	3·954	3·808	3·546	3·316	2·850	2·497	2·221	1·999
21	18·857	17·011	14·029	11·764	10·017	8·649	7·562	6·687	6·312	5·973	5·384	4·891	4·476	4·121	3·963	3·816	3·551	3·320	2·852	2·498	2·221	2·000
22	19·660	17·658	14·451	12·042	10·201	8·772	7·645	6·743	6·359	6·011	5·410	4·909	4·488	4·130	3·970	3·822	3·556	3·323	2·853	2·498	2·222	2·000
23	20·456	18·292	14·857	12·303	10·371	8·883	7·718	6·792	6·399	6·044	5·432	4·925	4·499	4·137	3·976	3·827	3·559	3·325	2·854	2·499	2·222	2·000
24	21·243	18·914	15·247	12·550	10·529	8·985	7·784	6·835	6·434	6·073	5·451	4·937	4·507	4·143	3·981	3·831	3·562	3·327	2·855	2·499	2·222	2·000
25	22·023	19·523	15·622	12·783	10·675	9·077	7·843	6·873	6·464	6·097	5·467	4·948	4·514	4·147	3·985	3·834	3·564	3·329	2·856	2·499	2·222	2·000
26	22·795	20·121	15·983	13·003	10·810	9·161	7·896	6·906	6·491	6·118	5·480	4·956	4·520	4·151	3·988	3·837	3·566	3·330	2·856	2·500	2·222	2·000
27	23·560	20·707	16·330	13·211	10·935	9·237	7·943	6·935	6·514	6·136	5·492	4·964	4·524	4·154	3·990	3·839	3·567	3·331	2·856	2·500	2·222	2·000
28	24·316	21·281	16·663	13·406	11·051	9·307	7·984	6·961	6·534	6·152	5·502	4·970	4·528	4·157	3·992	3·840	3·568	3·331	2·857	2·500	2·222	2·000
29	25·066	21·844	16·984	13·591	11·158	9·370	8·022	6·983	6·551	6·166	5·510	4·975	4·531	4·159	3·994	3·841	3·569	3·332	2·857	2·500	2·222	2·000
30	25·808	22·396	17·292	13·765	11·258	9·427	8·055	7·003	6·566	6·177	5·517	4·979	4·534	4·160	3·995	3·842	3·569	3·332	2·857	2·500	2·222	2·000
40	32·835	27·355	19·793	15·046	11·925	9·779	8·244	7·105	6·642	6·234	5·548	4·997	4·544	4·166	3·999	3·846	3·571	3·333	2·857	2·500	2·222	2·000
50	39·196	31·424	21·482	15·762	12·234	9·915	8·304	7·133	6·661	6·246	5·554	4·999	4·545	4·167	4·000	3·846	3·571	3·333	2·857	2·500	2·222	2·000

included in the final net cash flow. In the case of freehold land, where the value will not be lost in time and will in most cases exceed cost, the present value can be reduced to nil or even a minus quantity. This is because in such cases the net cash flow is required only to provide a return and nothing more, as the investment value will still be intact.

It should be noted that the net cash flow will not take into consideration any likely effect of inflation or changing money values unless this is taken into account when the amounts are computed in the first place. In the same way if it is anticipated that interest rates may vary over future years their effect should be taken into consideration when assessing the rate of return required.

LEASE OR BUY DECISIONS

The problem posed as regards fixed assets in this chapter has been the business decision involved in their purchase as opposed to non-purchase. However, in many cases of fixed-asset provision there is the associated problem of whether to purchase or lease the item concerned. These decisions may involve a further problem in that the buy or lease decision is dependent upon the replacement of an existing item. In this situation it is first necessary to determine whether or not to replace at all. This calculation will involve an assessment of the net cash flow to the capital invested if the old fixed asset is replaced by the purchase of a new one.

This calculation will be complicated by the fact that the cost of the new fixed asset will be reduced by any value which will be obtained from the sale of the existing fixed asset. The net cash flow will be computed from the savings applicable to the new fixed asset. If from this calculation it is found advisable to replace, the next consideration is to decide whether or not to buy or lease. In this calculation the cost of the new fixed asset will be measured against the savings which will be obtained from purchase as against leasing the item. These two steps are set out in the following illustrations:

A Ltd at present has a machine tool which is valued at £12,500. A new machine is available which will cost £49,000 and from which is expected a net saving over the old machine tool of £9,000 per annum over the next six years.

There is at present a company which will hire out a machine tool which will do the same job at an annual rental of £14,000 for a fixed period of five years. The hire contract provides for maintenance of the machine which will save the company £700 per annum if the machine is hired as opposed to being bought.

A Ltd looks for a return on fixed-asset investment of 12 per cent. Assume scrap value of new machine at end of five years nil.

Answer

It should be noted that, as the net cash flow is similar for each year, it will be possible to use the discount tables to determine the present value of £1 received annually for *N* years (see Table B, page 127).

STAGE I: FIND OUT WHETHER TO KEEP OR REPLACE

		£
Cost of New Machine		49,000
Less Scrap Value of Old Machine		12,500
		36,500

Net cash flow over 6 years = £9,000 × 4·111 = £36,999.
New machine will be purchased.

STAGE II: FIND OUT WHETHER TO HIRE OR BUY

Net cost of new machine £49,000 (as above).
Net cash flow = Saving if machine purchased as opposed to hired = (rent minus maintenance)

$$= £14,000 - £700 = £13,300$$

Net cash flow over 5 years = £13,300 × 3·605 = £47,947.
Savings of buying over hiring insufficient.
It is therefore worth replacing the old machine by hiring and not buying a new machine.

CONCLUSIONS

At the present time the method which is referred to as discounted cash flow is fast being adopted by most businesses using an investment-appraisal technique. It is, however, possible to combine this with the pay-back method and it is suggested that this is a very useful approach to this investment decision area. By using pay-back where it is applicable, as in the case of wasting assets subject to fast-changing technological development, it is possible to link the assessment of return obtained from the D.C.F. method with a measure of the time to pay back the original investment cost.

Finally, it is often believed by management that fixed-asset appraisal is a technique which should be applied only to large-scale investment in this area. In such cases the investment can be associated without effort with a corresponding net cash flow such as in the case of plant and machinery which will increase production output, resulting, when sold, in additional net income. This view ignores the fact that managers are concerned with a return on all the capital invested in the enterprise and this means a return on all the fixed assets. It is just as necessary to measure the profitable return on fixed assets such as a toilet in the factory or a typewriter in the office as it is on the new piece of plant and machinery.

The measure in such cases may not always be obvious in terms of additional net income, but it should be noted that a saving in typing time avoiding overtime payment or the preventing of a fine under the Factories Act for insufficient toilet facilities will have exactly the same financial result. It will also make management concern itself with examining all fixed-assets investments and will prevent the all-too-frequent situation of some being reviewed in detail and others being passed after the most cursory examination. All fixed assets should be equally examined and this means that all managers will be concerned with the appraisal techniques adopted by the business for whatever fixed assets come within their control.

Having established the method of appraisal each proposed investment will be presented to the capital-expenditure budget committee together with details of its cost and forecast net cash flow over the years ahead. In the case of accepted proposals it is vital that a progress system is used to verify the actual costs and the N.C.F. against the forecasts made. This step will deter the manager who decides to exaggerate the advantages of his proposals. This would be another duty of the budget officer referred to in the previous chapter.

Working Capital

Management's concern with working capital is to reduce this investment to the least amount necessary to carry on the trading activities of the business. This object is immediately understood by anyone wishing to start a business as he will recognize that if the capital needed for this area can be minimized the fixed-asset investment can be maximized.

THE PROBLEM

The result of this policy might be the difference between a shop in the High Street instead of one in a side road or a well-equipped factory as opposed to one with inadequate production facilities. To achieve this objective the manager must recognize the net nature of working capital. He must see it in all its different stages and understand why it is required in the first place. This understanding of its purpose is perhaps clearer to the manager at the start of his business operations than it may be once the enterprise is established. To define the need for working capital, it is necessary to understand each time within the cycle and to illustrate this we shall once more refer to the key diagram (see Fig. 10).

The working capital in this diagram is defined by the broken line and includes material in all its different stages of stock, including raw-material stock, and, if a manufacturing organization, work in

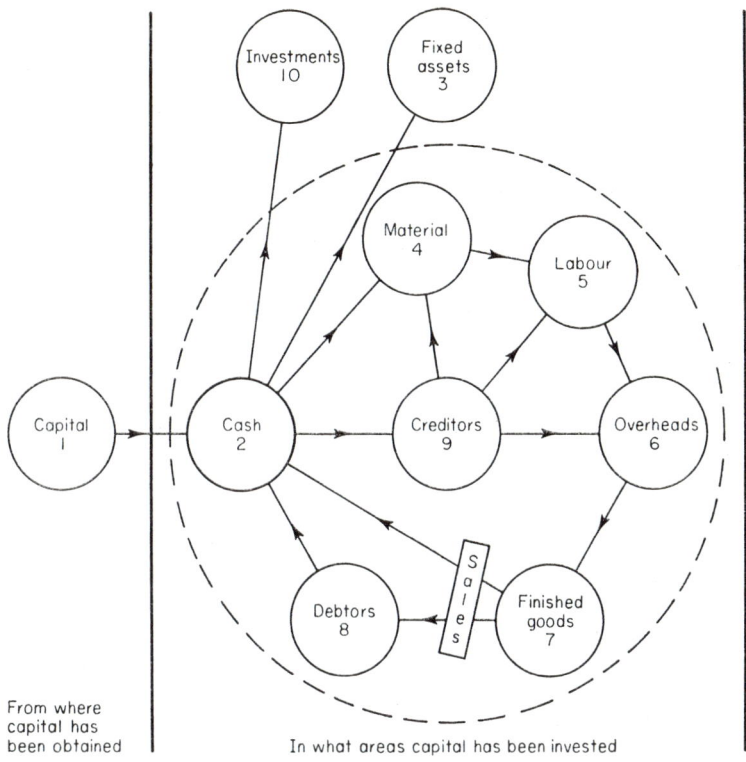

From where
capital has
been obtained

In what areas capital has been invested

FIGURE 10

progress and finished-goods stock, the raw-material value of which
will be increased by the appropriate labour and material costs which
have been incurred in production. In addition to stock values there
may be the need to allow customers to purchase goods on credit and
the amount due from such people, known as debtors, will require
to be financed. These are the items for which capital will be required
between cash being expended on materials, labour and overheads
and cash being received from the sales of goods or services. It must,
however, be understood that, in the case of each of these expense
items, credit will be allowed to the business by their suppliers of
material, labour and overheads termed creditors, and therefore to
compute working capital it is necessary to reduce the sum of the
stocks and debtors by the amounts due to suppliers of material,
labour and overheads. In the simplest terms working capital can be
defined as the capital required to bridge the gap between spending
money on producing the goods or services offered for sale by the

131

enterprise and receiving money back once these have been sold. It is the capital required to support the sales or turnover of the enterprise and could be expressed as so much per £ of sales. The recognition of the need to control this amount appears well understood by managers in the early days of any business. They see this gap and try to minimize it so as to free funds for fixed assets and to enable growth without diverting additional capital permanently into working capital. They also see that the size of this gap will be determined by one factor only—time: the time stock is held in its different stages; the time debtors take to pay for sales made to them; less the time taken by the business before paying for its material, labour and overheads. Working capital therefore represents a net time and the control and analysis of working capital involves the control and analysis of time. An understanding of this very simple fact is vital if any progress is to be made in this area of financial control.

WORKING CAPITAL ANALYSIS AND TIME

It should also be understood that all items in working capital are made up of one or all of the three expenses—material, labour and overheads. Stocks have already been defined in this manner earlier in the chapter, but this definition is equally true of debtors which represent unpaid-for sales. These are in respect of goods and services and thus the amount due is in respect of material, labour and overheads with, it is hoped or feared, the addition or subtraction of profit or loss. In the same way creditors refer to amounts due in respect of one expense or another.

CONTROL

The problem of working-capital control can therefore be seen as the need to maximize the speed or reduce the time between incurring the expense and receiving payment from the sales of the goods. Time is therefore of the essence and the need to obtain a speedy turnover of each expense item is vital in reducing the capital invested in this area.

However, although those concerned with enterprises in their early days understand this problem, this understanding is not always present in the long-established business. It would appear that once a business has reached a particular stage in its development, the necessary care and concern exercised by managers for capital involved in the working capital area seem to diminish. In the early days care is essential to conserve capital and each source and application is jealously controlled but this attitude has been known to disappear after the early strain is over. And yet, if progress is to be maintained or if advantage is to be made of a particular marketing situation, the need to control working capital is still of paramount importance. It is not by coincidence that the firm or firms which stand out as leaders in particular business areas are very often those who give more than normal attention to controlling this area of finance. An explanation of why the early vigilance over working-capital investment should be replaced by what might be termed slothful indifference may sometimes lie in the developing need for delegation. In the early stages of a business the management is often compact—being made up in some cases by as little as one, two or three senior managers. In these days the task of controlling time and tracing the progress of each expense from one stage to another can be done without great effort or far-stretched communications. This does not apply as the business grows and more and more delegation takes place. It will then be found that to control time in this area and to link one stage to the next becomes more and more difficult.

ILLUSTRATION OF WORKING CAPITAL CONTROL

So that we can examine the stages in which time must be controlled let us examine the following situation:

A Ltd is a manufacturing company producing chairs by means of batch production. An examination of records within the business shows that the following times are spent in the areas listed.

Average time at each stage

Raw material store	8 weeks
Production cycle	8 weeks (excl. parts stores)
Parts store	6 weeks
Finished goods store	4 weeks
Debtors	8 weeks
Credit received:	
Material	10 weeks
Labour	1 week
Overheads	4 weeks

From this it is possible to summarize the data so that each time element can be analysed into the progress stages as follows:

	Material Weeks	*Labour* Weeks	*Overheads* Weeks
Raw material store	8	—	8
Production cycle	8	8	8
Parts store	6	6	6
Finished goods store	4	4	4
Debtors	8	8	8
	34	26	34
Less: Credit	10	1	4
	24	25	30

133

In this summary time has been analysed into the several stages and under each expense head. It is assumed in the case of raw material store that the time spent there will tie up both material and overheads but not labour which would not be required during the time material is stored here. In the case of raw material the gross time between its arriving in the business and receiving the cash from the sales of units in which it is contained is 34 weeks. This is reduced by 10 weeks, representing the credit taken from suppliers, so in all 24 weeks of material will be invested in by this enterprise. For labour the gross amount is 26 weeks and this is reduced by 1 week to 25 weeks. The one week is the credit which is taken from employees if they are paid weekly. Overheads are tied up for a similar gross period to raw material but the reduction for creditors is only 4 weeks and so the net period is 30 instead of 24 weeks.

It should be noted that these data refer to A Ltd, and are not necessarily common to any other enterprise. In each case the relevant data must be found from inquiries within the particular business. From the summary of A Ltd it will be seen how each stage leads to the next one. For example, raw material store into the production cycle and from there via the parts store into the finished goods store. This flow also reflects a dependence which exists between each stage and it is important to understand this if we are to use these data in examining whether the time can be reduced.

THE CONTROL OF TIME
It must be remembered that a reduction of time in one stage, e.g. the production cycle, will not improve matters if this leads to extra time being required in storing finished goods. This point emphasizes the need for close liaison between all managers concerned with the control of working capital. In this respect let us examine each stage and note the managers who have some concern with the time element.

1 *Raw Material: Buyer and Production Manager*

The length of time material is stored will be affected by the buying policy. In certain cases this may be influenced by the production function where production planning requires large amounts of raw material to back it up.

2 *Production Cycle: Production Manager and Marketing Manager*

The time taken to produce the goods will be determined in most cases by the production management, but this may be affected to some degree by sales if they are not co-ordinated with production planning.

134

3 Parts: Store as for Production Cycle

This time is controlled similarly to that for the production cycle and indicates that sales and production planning are not totally co-ordinated until the finishing stages.

4 Finished Goods Store: Production Manager and Sales Manager

The time taken to store finished goods will be determined in most cases by the marketing function, but if production does not fulfil the sales needs the time will be influenced by this function.

5 Debtors: Finance Manager and Sales Manager

It is usual to consider the time taken in this area to be the responsibility of the financial function and in particular the credit controller. However, it may be found if credit sales are made without any reference to the financial standing of customers that the sales function is a very significant contributory factor to the time taken in his area.

6 Creditors: Financial Manager and Buyer

The time taken by a business before paying amounts due for material, labour and overheads is not always determinable by any particular function. For instance, the credit taken of one month or one week in respect of salaries and wages. However, the credit taken before paying for material suppliers and certain overhead items is negotiable and may be varied by those directly responsible for the purchase of these items—in most cases these will be the buying and financial managers.

CONTROL CONCLUSIONS

On an examination of each of those items which make up working capital three points should be kept in mind:

(i) the way in which each amount is regulated by more than one manager in many cases;

(ii) the interdependence of one item and another as already referred to; and

(iii) the absence in most areas of this investment of the supervision by a manager directly connected with the financial function—in fact, apart from debtors and creditors such a manager has no direct part to play.

This last point means that if this area of investment is to be adequately controlled its importance must be fully understood by all managers irrespective of their specific function. This will call for a thorough knowledge of the effects of this investment and for very close co-operation between one function and another. It is perhaps this need for understanding and co-operation which lies at the root of the problem but the difficulty is worsened as the enterprise grows and communication becomes more stretched.

WORKING CAPITAL SAVINGS
To return to the previous illustration, if we were to assemble some further facts regarding A Ltd it would be possible to convert the time quantities so far produced into the amounts of working capital which will be required at different levels of turnover. For instance, if it is forecast that over the next twelve months the sales will be £4,000,000 and that the material, labour and overheads cost will be 40, 30 and 20 per cent respectively of sales value, the costs of these three expense items can be computed as follows:

$$\text{Material:} \quad \frac{40}{100} \times £4{,}000{,}000 = £1{,}600{,}000$$

$$\text{Labour:} \quad \frac{30}{100} \times £4{,}000{,}000 = 1{,}200{,}000$$

$$\text{Overhead costs:} \quad \frac{20}{100} \times £4{,}000{,}000 = 800{,}000$$

$$\underline{£3{,}600{,}000}$$

The total cost will therefore be £3,600,000 for the year if all is in accordance with the forecast and the weeks calculated for each expense item can be converted into financial quantities as follows:

$$\text{Material:} \quad \frac{24}{50} \times £1{,}600{,}000 = £768{,}000$$

$$\text{Labour:} \quad \frac{25}{50} \times £1{,}200{,}000 = 600{,}000$$

$$\text{Overheads:} \quad \frac{30}{50} \times £800{,}000 = 480{,}000$$

$$\underline{£1{,}848{,}000}$$

It must be recognized that these calculations are all based on an average situation and no reliance can be placed upon their accuracy within the nearest £1–2,000. However, as an indication, the data will prove invaluable and will certainly highlight the connection of time and money. We have now calculated (*a*) the time involved in the present production, selling and financial policies of A Ltd in the area of working capital and (*b*) the cost of this time in terms of working capital investment.

Now let us examine the effect of saving of time and in this calculation we shall assume a saving of 4 weeks in the parts store. This will save 4 weeks in each expense and from the data the effect on working capital can be calculated as follows:

$$\text{Material:} \qquad \frac{4}{50} \times £1,600,000 = £128,000$$

$$\text{Labour:} \qquad \frac{4}{50} \times £1,200,000 = 96,000$$

$$\text{Overheads:} \qquad \frac{4}{50} \times £800,000 = 64,000$$

$$\frac{4}{50} \times £3,600,000 = £288,000$$

A saving therefore of £288,000 in the investment would be provided and this could be diverted into any other investment in the business. Or it might be put into investments outside the enterprise and even given a small return of 8 per cent per annum would bring in £23,040 annually.

THE USE OF SAVINGS

Savings are calculated only up to this stage, although in the case of a parts store the floor area no longer required to store the parts might be included as a rent saving and this rather theoretical saving added to the interest on reinvested capital. However, there is another way of considering savings in this area. Suppose A Ltd in the example has available fixed assets, i.e. production capacity, to produce more of its products and these if made could be sold in the year in question. If this situation applies then the £288,000 working capital saving, arising from the elimination of the parts store, could be used to finance additional sales. This, after all, is the purpose of working capital investment: to finance or support sales.

To return to the illustration, it was first calculated that A Ltd required £1,848,000 to support sales of £4,000,000 or that for every £1 sales A Ltd would require £0·462. The saving of £288,000 reduces working capital needs from £1,848,000 to £1,560,000 and this would equal a requirement of £0·39 for every £1. The saved £288,000 would therefore reduce the working capital needs from 46 to 39p per £1 of sales and the total saving would support additional sales calculated as follows:

$$\frac{£288,000}{0·39} = £740,000 \text{ approx.}$$

The net profit on sales is 10 per cent (100 per cent minus materials 40 per cent, labour 30 per cent and overheads 20 per cent) and this will therefore be £74,000 per annum.

This is considerably in excess of the £23,040 calculated on the outside investment of the saved capital and would represent a return on the capital saved of approximately 25 per cent. It also ignores any rental saving, if any, which might also occur.

This use of saved working capital as the spring-board from which to launch an increased sales drive without the need for additional working capital funds is the dynamic approach to this problem. Savings in this area of investment will cost money, because of the need either to provide better management, i.e. a better buyer who will negotiate more advantageous credit terms with suppliers, or to introduce control technique which will require staffing and service, e.g. production control to reduce time in the production cycle and the parts store. Nevertheless, if these savings will bring about expansion such as that illustrated above, the costs of the new managers or techniques have got to be very considerable indeed before they become unprofitable. Certainly, the statements that if we save the time of storing raw material "we shall lose the bulk discounts and other favourable buying terms" or if we save in other stores areas "we will only save the rental and even that is doubtful" can soon be dismissed if we consider the additional profits on additional sales which can or might be achieved by the use of the freed working capital to support sales. Even in the case of an enterprise which cannot divert such funds into supporting additional sales owing to either a lack of demand for its goods or a restriction on its production capacity, the reduction should still be made. The reason for this is that when the opportunity does arise to expand sales, the enterprise will not be prevented from taking advantage of the situation owing to excess working capital need per £1 of sales.

CONCLUSIONS

It is suggested that this area of investment is the foundation of any expanding enterprise and it is to this area that the management must look in times of growth. For this reason, its care and control is fundamental to all managers and their contribution must be explained and emphasized. It is vital that joint discussions are held between buying, production, sales and financial managers to examine possible time savings in each area and their conversion into financial savings. Those who present working capital information should avoid the jargon of the balance sheet which can have a distracting effect upon those concerned with its control. For instance, working capital on a balance sheet is described as current assets less current liabilities and each item can be traced to the now familiar key diagram. However, for the purpose of financial presentation it may be found expedient to include items in current assets or current liabilities which do not always fit into the terms of working capital as described in this chapter. For example, cash or near cash is included in current assets. These items are considered current assets as there is no reason at the balance-sheet date to assume that they are fixed assets and the likelihood is that they will be reinvested in the working-capital cycle. It is, however, more a matter of financial convenience to present such items as current assets than to define the sums involved as being needed as working capital. It will also be noted that in the illustration on this subject set out on page 136, the working capital needs were calculated strictly in accordance with data supplied and no margin was included for a possible need of cash in any unforeseeable circumstance. If it were felt necessary to provide for this situation it would be quite in order to increase the total working capital calculated by any amount which was considered necessary.

The fact that presenters of financial information treat uninvested cash or temporary investments as part of the working capital may highlight the need for controlling this area of investment. It indicates that, whenever funds are available, they will be diverted into working capital and this indeed is very often the case in practice. It has certainly been found that where uncontrolled or undisciplined investment takes place in a business it often takes the form of over-high stocks at all levels or of debtors being allowed to take excessive credit or even of credit not being taken when it is possible. This diversion of funds is often due to lazy and uncoordinated management, as this excess investment lessens the need for control and insulates each manager against the effect of his own inefficiency. For example, the buyer is never caught without any particular raw material as it is always there, even if difficult to find! The salesmen never have to explain away the over-zealous action of the credit controllers. It has, however, been my ill-fortune to record a working capital in one business with which I was familiar of 80p per £ of sales which made growth fairly unlikely however propitious the market conditions.

It follows from this that the provision of working capital funds is normally traceable to retained earnings. This source is the most convenient and it is often found difficult to raise funds from shareholders and long-term lenders for this purpose. Funds obtained from these sources are in most cases earmarked for fixed-asset investment and it is normally found that working capital is provided out of retained profits. This is a very reasonable approach to fund-raising, but if excess investment is being made in working capital it will follow that more profits are being retained than are strictly required. This point will be further developed in the next chapter.

Finally, there can be cases of fixed-asset investment which will call for supporting working capital. This will occur when there is a working-capital need to support sales and the proposed fixed asset will increase the sales volume of the business. In such cases the additional working capital should be included with the cost of the fixed asset so as to compute the true investment cost against which to assess the net cash flow.

6   *Cash Flow*

In the first chapter we described the setting up of a business in financial terms. We discussed the provision of capital and its investment in either fixed assets or working capital and arising from this we showed the development of financial information. At this stage we were discussing capital being injected into the business as cash and the decisions regarding investment involved in the spending of cash.

The financial centre of any new business is cash but this is equally true as the business develops. Any examination of a business must include a review of the cash movement so as to show both the sources of cash and its application in the business. For this reason there has developed a series of information statements describing the flow of cash within the business. Such statements deal with both the source of cash and its application, and these two aspects will be considered in this chapter.

SOURCES OF CASH

So as to understand this subject fully we should first consider the several sources of capital which are available to a business. No business can exist without capital and this commodity in its raw state will be cash. The permanent cash required to start a business, termed initial permanent capital, will be introduced from two main sources, namely:

    (i) proprietor's capital;
    (ii) long-term loans.

In the case of limited companies these sources become share issues and long-term loans in the form of mortgages and debentures.

Retained Profits

When a business is formed it will require permanent capital and this will be obtained from the two sources described above. In most cases it will be found that additional permanent capital will be required and this will certainly be so if fixed assets need to be added to or working capital requirements are increased. In these circumstances recourse can be had to the two areas of capital provision already described but in most cases a gradual increase in needs is met from capital obtained from retained profits.

Profit is reflected in additional capital which has been invested in the enterprise in the same way as losses reflect a reduction of capital investment.

Profit retention is the major source of additional capital in many businesses and the planning of profits—their making and keeping—is as vital as the planning of shares or debenture issues. This source of cash has been dealt with in Chapter 2.

THE APPLICATION OF CASH

When the capital has been obtained from one of the sources detailed above, we must now consider how this cash will be invested in the enterprise. To illustrate this, let us examine the situation set out below:

A Ltd started business on 1 January 19.. with cash of £500,000

BALANCE SHEET

As at 1 January 1971

		£
SHARE CAPITAL		500,000
FIXED ASSETS:		
Freehold land and buildings	£200,000	
Plant and machinery	150,000	
Furniture and fittings	40,000	
		390,000
WORKING CAPITAL:		
Current Assets		
Stock of Raw Material	160,000	
Less: Current Liabilities		
Creditors	50,000	
		110,000
		500,000

142

which it obtained by issuing ordinary shares of £1 each. The directors of the company invested this amount as follows:

Freehold land and buildings = £200,000.
Plant and machinery = £150,000.
Furniture and fittings = £40,000.
Stocks of raw material = £160,000, of which £50,000 of the raw material was bought on credit.

From this information the opening balance sheet would appear as shown on page 142.

This balance sheet sets out the source and application of capital and it also describes the movement of cash or the cash flow in the

A LTD
BALANCE SHEET
As at 31 December 1971

						£
SHARE CAPITAL	.	.	.	.	.	550,000
RESERVES:						
Share premium	.	.	.	.	.	10,000
General reserve	.	.	.	.	.	20,000
Profit & loss account	.	.	.	.		30,000
TAXATION RESERVE	.	.	.	.	.	15,000
LONG-TERM LOAN	.	.	.	.	.	10,000
						635,000

FIXED ASSETS				Cost	Deprecia-tion	£
Freehold land and buildings	.	.	.	£220,000	—	220,000
Plant and machinery	.	.	.	170,000	£30,000	140,000
Furniture & fittings .	.	.	.	40,000	8,000	32,000
Motor vehicles	.	.	.	30,000	11,000	19,000
				460,000	49,000	411,000

INVESTMENT IN B LTD	.	.	.	.			100,000
WORKING CAPITAL							
Current Assets:							
Stocks	.	.	.	.	.	£220,000	
Debtors	.	.	.	.	.	80,000	
Cash	.	.	.	.	.	6,000	
						£306,000	
Less: Current Liabilities:							
Creditors .	.	.	.	.	.	£176,500	
Proposed Dividend	.	.	.	.		5,500	
						182,000	
							124,000
							£635,000

company. From an investment viewpoint an examination of cash movement or flow highlights the supervision exercised by management over this commodity. This becomes increasingly important as the business progresses, because the cash movement which is clear on the opening balance sheet as in A Ltd above is less obvious as time goes by owing to the manner of balance sheet presentation. To illustrate this point we shall now consider the balance sheet of A Ltd after it has traded for twelve months (see page 143).

The balance sheet at 1 January can be converted into a statement showing the movement of cash without much adjustment, as follows:

CASH IN £500,000

CASH INVESTED:
Fixed assets £390,000
Working capital 110,000

£500,000

However, in the case of the balance sheet as at 31 December, a statement of cash in and how it has been invested is not so simple and certain adjustments will be necessary which are shown and discussed below:

CASH INTO BUSINESS

	£	£
SHARE CAPITAL	550,000	

RETAINED PROFITS:
Share premium	£10,000	
General reserves	20,000	
Taxation reserve	15,000	
Profit & loss account	30,000	
Depreciation	49,000	
Proposed dividend	5,500	
Long-term loans	10,000	
		139,500
		689,500

CASH INVESTED IN BUSINESS
Fixed Assets	£460,000	
Investment in B Ltd	100,000	
Working Capital	129,500	
		689,500

Cash has come into the business from the following sources:

Share Capital: This figure of £550,000 has been increased from the item shown at 1 January as the result of an issue of additional shares.

Retained Profits: As previously explained, whenever profits are retained within a business this will result in an increase in capital which represents cash available for investment. In the case of A Ltd profits have been retained by the premium payable on the shares issued to the amount of £10,000 and in addition to this retained profits have been increased by £20,000 and £30,000 under the heads of general reserve and profit and loss account. Profits have also been retained to meet the future taxation payment of £15,000 and to provide for depreciation of £49,000 for the future need to replace the cost of fixed assets. Neither of these last two items has resulted in the payment of cash out of the business and therefore the cash represented is still invested within the enterprise. This fact is equally true of the proposed dividend of £5,500; so this is also added back as a source of cash within the business stemming from retained profits.

Long-term Loans: Finally, £10,000 has been received from investors who have lent moneys to the concern on a long-term basis.

Creditors: This item might also be included as a source of cash as it has enabled additional investment in fixed assets and/or current assets. However, in the illustration the amount of £176,500 has been deducted from current assets to show a net investment of cash in working capital of £129,500.

Cash Movement Summary

The total cash which is now invested in A Ltd is £689,500 and this has been invested as described in the illustration. The statement above illustrating cash in no way pinpoints a period. It describes the cash that has been received and retained in the business since its commencement and how such cash has been invested. However, as period follows period the investors and managers become concerned with changes or movements in cash within the period under review and for this reason seek a summary which will illustrate this situation.

To show this need let us consider A Ltd for the period to 31 December on the assumption that the balance sheet on 1 January has been thoroughly understood by the investors and manager of the business. In this situation the need is to know the additional cash that has flowed into the business during the year to 31 December—since the initial injection of £500,000—and to learn exactly where such funds have been invested. From this information the rationale of the investment policy of A Ltd's management can be thoroughly reviewed by all concerned.

SUMMARY OF ADDITIONAL CASH
For Period to 31 December 19. .

		£	£
SHARE CAPITAL		50,000	
RETAINED PROFITS:			
Share premium	£10,000		
General reserves	20,000		
Profit and loss account	30,000		
Taxation reserve	15,000		
Depreciation	49,000		
Proposed dividend	5,500		
		129,500	
Long-term loan		10,000	
			189,500

APPLICATION OF FUNDS:		
Fixed assets	70,000	
Investment in B Ltd	100,000	
Working capital	19,500	
		189,500

From this statement it will be seen that during this period the managers have had a further £189,500 to invest within the business. With this amount they have increased investment in fixed assets by £70,000, investments in B Ltd by £100,000 and working capital by £19,500.

The fresh summaries of a balance sheet made in the way described above provide a detailed view of the source and application of cash and this method could be expanded in detail to show each individual item of investment that has taken place such as stock as opposed to debtors, etc.

The summary of cash movement described above is the starting point for a review of investment in any business. Every manager must be concerned with the cash resources under his control and a review of how this commodity has been dealt with during any period becomes highly relevant.

Problems of Cash Control

To implement any control over the cash resources and therefore to control the cash flow, it is necessary to set out clearly the manner in which cash will be applied within the enterprise. This need becomes very marked when it is considered that in many businesses, and certainly in the case of A Ltd illustrated above, the major source of cash is retained profits.

Whenever cash is received from share capital or long-term loan issues as well as retained profits there will be a need to decide how the cash will be invested. In the two former cases, the cash will be received in one sum and its application will await its arrival, that is it will await the receipt of cash payable by the shareholders or long-term lenders. However, in the case of retained profits this item will arise in the business throughout the period in which profits are made and decisions as to its use will have to be taken during this time.

Cash Flow and Net Profit Retained

In addition to this continuous source problem which relates to cash derived from retained profits, there is also the difficulty that expenses and income shown in the profit and loss statement do not always coincide with the actual cash payments and receipts. This latter problem was dealt with in Chapter 4 under cash budgeting and it is indeed most necessary for those concerned with the application of cash into the several areas of fixed assets, working capital and outside investment to co-ordinate this with cash budgeting. Such budgets should be scaled down to periods of control such as weeks or months and this will then reflect how profits made and retained will swell the liquid resources available for investment within the enterprise.

Profits retained which will be represented as additional cash for investment within the business has been described as a "sneaky" source of capital. This may be an unfair generalization, but it is certainly true that, where there is unprofitable investment within an enterprise, its source is often found to be retained profits. It is suggested that the reason for this is that, whilst in the case of share capital and long-term loans the cash derived from these sources will be invested in projects described in detail to the investors and as such guaranteed a reasonable return, in the case of retained profits, little mention will be made regarding how the funds will be applied. In fact, retained profits are often simply mentioned in such terms as "The company has decided to place £x into a general reserve", or "£y into a reserve for the increased cost of replacing fixed assets". Such statements have no meaning as to where the cash represented by the retained profits will be invested within the concern. To meet this problem it is important that both managers and investors are kept informed not only as to the amount of additional cash obtained from retained profits of all descriptions, but also as to the application of such funds. For this reason, there is a real need to present in addition to a profit and loss statement and balance sheet, a cash-flow analysis, especially where the majority of additional capital stems from this area.

CASH FLOW ILLUSTRATION

For a fuller examination of the source and application of cash funds, it is now necessary to examine a more detailed profit and loss statement and balance sheet, together with certain supporting data. From this information we shall then examine the different ways in which the cash flow can be presented to managers and investors.

The three cash flow statements (pages 150, 151, 152) set out in varying detail the movement of cash within A Ltd during the period under review. Each item should be studied by the reader, together with the contents of this chapter, so that they can be fully understood.

The first statement makes no real attempt to interpret the data. It simply takes the differences between the information for the current and previous periods and presents them under each head.

The second statement concentrates on summarizing without explanation. This may produce a neat statement, but it is difficult to take any action until further data are available.

PROFIT & LOSS ACCOUNT

Year ended 31 December 19..

TRADING PROFIT—after charging:		£225,000
Directors' emoluments	£40,000	
Depreciation:		
Leasehold land & buildings	£50,000	
Plant & machinery	70,000	
Office equipment	10,000	
Trade investments	2,000	
	132,000	
Corporation tax		65,000
Profit after corporation tax		160,000
Balance c/fwd from previous year		120,000
		280,000
Transfer to capital reserve	£50,000	
„ „ general reserve	50,000	
Proposed dividend	25,000	
		125,000
		155,000

A LTD
BALANCE SHEET
As at 31 December 1971

Capital and Liabilities

1970 £		Authorized (All £1 Shares) £	Issued & Fully Paid £	£
	SHARE CAPITAL			
100,000	7% Redeemable preference shares	250,000	100,000	
50,000	6% preference shares	200,000	100,000	
1,100,000	Ordinary shares	1,500,000	1,200,000	
1,250,000		1,950,000	1,400,000	1,400,000
	RESERVES	£		£
100,000	Capital Redemption reserve fund	100,000		
—	Share premium account	100,000		
50,000	Capital reserve	50,000	250,000	
55,000	General reserve	105,000		
120,000	Profit & loss account	155,000	260,000	
1,400,000			510,000	1,910,000
100,000	6% Debentures		200,000	
1,675,000				2,110,000
	Corporation tax			65,000
	CURRENT LIABILITIES	£		
210,000	Creditors	320,000		
40,000	Accruals	38,000		
60,000	Bank overdraft	40,000		
18,000	Dividends proposed	25,000		
328,000			423,000	
2,003,000				**£2,598,000**

Assets

	COST £	DEPRECIATION TO DATE £	£	1970 £
FIXED ASSETS				
Freehold land & buildings	1,000,000	—	1,000,000	600,000
Leasehold land & buildings	500,000	350,000	150,000	200,000
Plant & machinery	852,000	420,000	432,000	500,000
Office equipment	95,000	62,000	33,000	40,000
Trade investments	70,000	6,000	64,000	66,000
	2,517,000	838,000	1,679,000	1,406,000
Investment in B Ltd, at Cost			350,000	150,000
			2,029,000	1,556,000
CURRENT ASSETS	£			
Raw material stock	120,000			80,000
Work in progress stock	105,000			65,000
Finished goods stock	117,000			100,000
Prepayments	14,000			18,000
Debtors	210,000			183,900
Bank	2,100			
Cash	900			100
			569,000	447,000
			£2,598,000	**£2,003,000**

A LTD
CASH FLOW STATEMENT I
19../19..

	£	£
ADDITIONAL CASH		
SHARE CAPITAL:		
6% Preference Shares	50,000	
Ordinary Shares	100,000	
		150,000
Share premium		50,000
Capital reserve		50,000
General reserve		50,000
Profit & loss account		35,000
Taxation reserve		65,000
Debentures		100,000
Depreciation		132,000
Creditors		110,000
Dividends proposed		7,000
Reductions in current assets prepayment		4,000
		753,000

	£	£
USE OF CASH		
REDUCTION IN CURRENT LIABILITIES:		
Accruals	2,000	
Bank overdraft	20,000	
		22,000
INCREASE IN FIXED ASSETS:		
Freehold property	400,000	
Plant & machinery	2,000	
Office equipment	3,000	
		405,000
Increase in investment in B Ltd		200,000
INCREASE IN CURRENT ASSETS:		
Raw material stock	40,000	
Work in progress stock	40,000	
Finished goods stock	17,000	
Debtors	26,100	
Bank	2,000	
Cash	900	
		126,000
		753,000

150

CASH FLOW STATEMENT II
19../19..

ADDITIONS TO CASH	£
Share capital	150,000
Retained profits	382,000
Long-term loans	100,000
	632,000

USE OF CASH	£
Fixed assets	405,000
Investments outside business	200,000
Working capital	27,000
	632,000

The third statement (see page 152) summarizes the cash flow with an accent upon explaining the reason behind it and thus providing a rationale of the investment policy of the organization.

From the data presented it will be necessary to explain the increased investment in freeholds, investment in B Ltd, and the stock, debtors and creditors increases. The reason may be that a freehold factory has been purchased and, although production has begun to expand because of this increased production capacity, its full effect has still to be felt. This might explain the stock and debtor increases and the rise in creditors. The investment in B Ltd will need to be explained separately. The cash-flow statement will highlight all investment changes, both inside and outside the business, and this, it is suggested, will create in itself a discipline upon management. It is believed that there is a very real need for all businesses to produce a cash-flow summary to highlight the source and application of cash resources. Such statements will show managers the cash effect of their actions during periods under review and will also lead to far more informative reviews of companies' investment policies for investors and the general public.

OVERTRADING

The co-ordination of cash resources with investment needs lies at the root of successful business progress and expansion. In the same way as with a private individual it is vital to make sure that when there is a need for liquid funds these are available. If such financial co-ordination is lacking, a situation may well be created which is termed "overtrading" and which must be fully understood by all

151

CASH FLOW STATEMENT III
19../19..

ADDITIONS TO CASH

		£	£
SHARE CAPITAL:			
6% Preference Shares	. . . .	50,000	
Ordinary Shares	. . . . .	100,000	
			150,000
RETAINED PROFITS:			
Share premium	. . . . .		50,000
Trading profit	. . . . .	225,000	
Add: Depreciation	. . . .	132,000	
		357,000	
Less: Dividend	. . . . .	25,000	
			332,000
6% Debentures	. . . . . .		100,000
			£632,000

USE OF CASH

		£	£
FIXED ASSETS:			
Freehold property	. . . . .	400,000	
Plant & machinery	. . . . .	2,000	
Office equipment	. . . . .	3,000	
			405,000
Increase in Investment in B Ltd	. . .		200,000
WORKING CAPITAL:			
Current Assets:			
Raw material stock	. . . .	40,000	
Work in progress stock	. . .	40,000	
Finished goods stock	. . . .	17,000	
Debtors & prepayments	. . .	22,100	
Bank & cash	. . . . .	2,900	
		122,000	
Less: Current Liabilities:			
Creditors & accruals	. . . .	108,000	
Bank overdraft reduction	. . .	20,000	
Dividend	. . . . . .	7,000	
		95,000	
			27,000
			£632,000

managers so that its dangers can be recognized and avoided. Overtrading can be defined as trading with insufficient liquid funds. This situation makes it necessary to act financially in a particular manner and it is this action which damages the enterprise. For this reason it is most important to avoid overtrading and the resulting action. An example of overtrading can be illustrated by referring back to the key diagram:

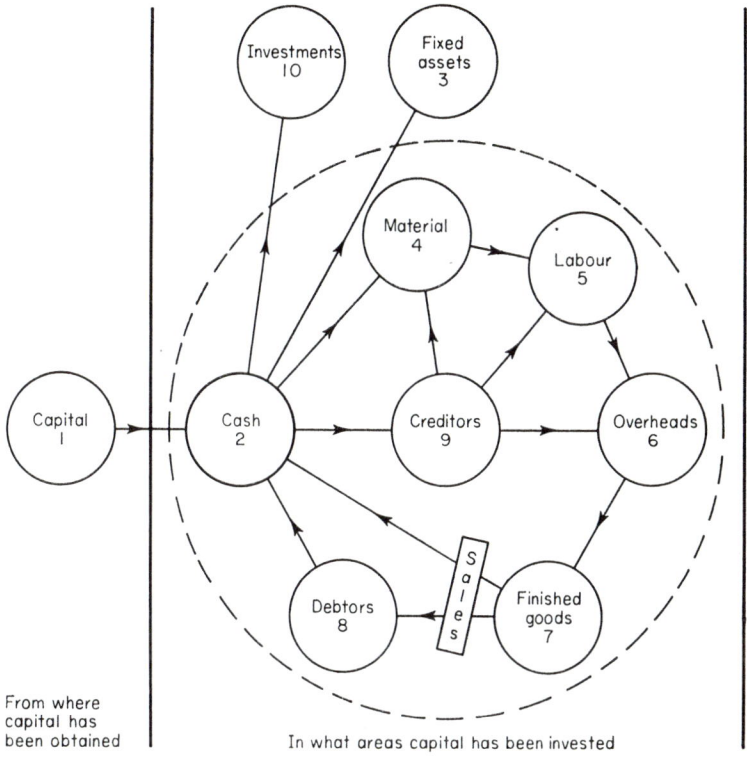

FIGURE 11

Business Expansion

Suppose the above diagram refers to a company known as A Ltd. This company decides to expand its trading activities, which sets up the following financial situation. To support the expansion more material, labour and overheads will be required, and as A Ltd sells its goods on credit the debtors will increase in line with the expansion. It is assumed that fixed assets will be adequate for the expansion, but if this were not so, these would also require additional investment. Together with this increased investment the amount of credit taken from suppliers of materials, labour and overheads will increase, although the time taken before payment should still be in accordance with the trade practice. Given these circumstances,

153

A Ltd will continue its expansion plans, but let us suppose there is a delay, which is probable, between building up to the level of increased turnover and receiving the benefit from this in the return of cash from additional sales. The action which the management must take if it has no spare liquid resources will be similar to that which everyone personally must take when faced with a similar situation. They must either seek assistance from a bank or other lending source or delay payment. In most situations of this kind, the time required to arrange borrowing is too long and so payment delay takes place. From this action certain loss-creating factors may take place. For instance, any cash discounts will be lost. Also material suppliers will be concerned at having to await the moneys due and this may lead to fresh supplies of material being delivered in a less efficient way, leading to losses created by production delays and additional inspection needs.

Overtrading Action

In addition to action which is taken to delay payment of cash in these circumstances action may also be taken to speed up the receipt of cash by encouraging debtors to pay before their normal credit term. To stimulate such action it will normally be necessary to offer increased cash discount terms, which will again add a further loss factor. It will be seen, therefore, that overtrading has necessitated action which has led to losses. Whether or not these losses will cancel out the profits gained through the expansion of trade will depend upon all the circumstances of the enterprise, but it should be noted that an expanding business is often working on very small margins. Such margins are necessary for expansion and the loss factors mentioned above may well be enough to wipe out the anticipated profits of the business and may in fact lead into a total net-loss position. This situation which results from over-trading is a constant fear of those concerned with providing funds for expansion, such as bankers. Their fear is that in providing such funds they will enable a business to begin its expansion programme but if such funds are insufficient the end-result could well be over-trading with its attendant consequences. For this reason, it is important for any expansion plans to be accompanied by a full cash forecast. This forecast must be laid out in detail for each period with, say, monthly rests as illustrated on page 105 in the case of cash budgets. By having these data available, it will be possible to see whether the expansion is feasible from a liquid point of view and if not to see well before such expansion takes place whether it is possible to negotiate additional cash funds. It is far wiser to seek

154

overdraft facilities well before they are needed than to find the need upon you before any arrangements have been negotiated.

Avoidance of Overtrading

It should be noted that when seeking financial assistance in an expansion situation it is wiser to ask for all that is possibly required than to limit the request to a point which does not cover every contingency. It is so often found in business as in private life that original forecasts of cash needs are greatly under-estimated and it is most important when estimating needs to allow for every possible contingency.

Finally, it should be noted that overtrading is a problem that affects the expanding and progressive organization and all managers must ensure that their own organization is not affected. The difference between success and failure in such situations may well be the availability of cash. Without this commodity decisions are made such as extending credit taken from suppliers and reducing credit given to customers which lead inevitably to losses but which are themselves made inevitable owing to the overtrading position.

CONCLUSION

Cash lies at the centre of investment. It forms the base of every business in whatever stage of development it may be. For this reason every manager requires a review of cash movement both into and around the enterprise and in a situation of expansion the problems associated with overtrading must be fully understood.

7 Interpretation and Use of Financial Information

So far this book has dealt with the financial information which can be made available to managers. From balance sheets and profit and loss statements have been traced all the supporting and explanatory financial techniques which have been developed to answer the inquiring manager's questions. But once the data are presented we are left with the need to interpret and understand.

In this we must be aware of three facts regarding the information:

    (i) what information is being presented;
    (ii) how the information has been compiled; and
    (iii) what can be learned from the information.

Once we have determined these facts we can proceed with interpretation—but not until then. To understand these steps, let us examine each point in detail.

What Information Is Being Presented

The need to know what information is being presented has been emphasized throughout this text. Nevertheless, it is suggested that much of the lack of understanding of data stems from a failure to recognize what is being presented.

DEFINITION OF TERMS
This failure is often traceable to not understanding the limitations of the data, for instance, costings based on historical values, fixed assets presented at cost, stocks at cost or market value on balance sheets.

In recent years the difficulty in which this lack of definition places the investor in the case of published accounts has been given considerable notice both in the national and investment press, and this is causing real concern in the accountancy world itself. Much of the criticism has been directed towards the situations which arise through a lack of clarity on the basis of valuation which should be adopted when presenting information.

This absence of definition can lead to the presentation of completely different values for the same item in a particular business, with most misleading results. For example, stocks might be shown based on the material, labour and full overhead value of each item or the value might be confined simply to materials, labour and other variable expense costs. The difference between these two amounts for the identical items might well be considerable in a large concern and would have a corresponding effect upon the information shown on the balance sheet.

The controversy regarding financial information is at present being closely considered by the accountancy profession and it is hoped that during the next few years a series of agreed bases of values and methods of presentation will be adopted by those concerned with such statements.

However, it will not be possible for such definitions to embrace all areas of financial data owing to the volume and diversity of these within different organizations. It is therefore essential that each enterprise should prepare its own definitions regarding the basis of valuation of financial data. It is suggested that each firm should produce a glossary or dictionary which would assist in this difficulty. This glossary would define first, clearly and simply, what each piece of financial information being presented was. Second, it would define the basis of valuation of each item and this should be done with great care and clarity of expression so that everyone would be able to understand without the necessity of previous financial training.

The manager should know not only the type and variety of the information presented but also the manner and basis of its presentation. The basis of valuation of items presented must be such that the limitation of the data can be understood and the interpretation brought within this scale.

From experience it has been found that within any information system much wastage occurs through a lack of understanding as to what is available. This can lead to duplication where certain data are produced in parallel outside the system. The glossary or dictionary of available data might well make it possible to avoid such duplication.

How the Information Has Been Compiled and How It Can Be Used

Having clearly established what is available and the basis upon which each piece of data has been produced, the need to know how it is compiled becomes apparent. A thorough understanding and use of data presupposes an understanding of its construction as much as first-class driving presupposes a basic knowledge of mechanics. Without such understanding, it is difficult to see how a manager can check whether or not the information is being presented on time, or whether it would be possible to produce the data more speedily or at a more convenient date. An understanding of the construction of each financial statement enables managers to see the interconnection of one piece of data with another. For this reason, it might prove useful to include an explanation of how the information has been compiled in the glossary referred to in the previous section. This all-round knowledge of financial information is the foundation of all interpretation and understanding. Without this it is difficult to use the data and much will be lost in its full understanding.

Glossary of Financial Information

The use of a financial information dictionary or glossary should be adopted by all enterprises. This should contain full references to the following points:

1 The financial information being presented within the enterprise. To whom it is presented. When it is presented. Why it is presented.

2 The basis of valuation of each item presented within the enterprise.

3 How the information is presented. From what source the data are compiled. When the information is presented.

This information must be kept up to date and expanded whenever it is necessary. This glossary should include definitions of terms which may be found difficult by those not trained in finance.

The dictionary might be used to define all information systems within the concern, whether or not they relate to the financial function. Examples of these are work study, production control or marketing data. By this reference system, it might well be found possible to assist managers to digest the ever-increasing volume of business communications and also prevent the all-too-familiar problem of data duplication referred to above.

THE EXAMINATION OF FINANCIAL INFORMATION

We shall now examine financial information presented to managers in the light of its interpretation. In this examination we shall concentrate upon three main aspects of each piece of information, namely its limitation, its main use and its supplementary use.

LIMITATION
The limitation of financial data has already been referred to in the introduction to this chapter. It can refer to the basis of valuation as illustrated, or it could refer to such facts as the clerical cost of data preparation or to its historical nature. Whatever are its limitations, they must be clearly understood by managers when presented with information. A failure to recognize these can lead to grossly incorrect conclusions being drawn by a manager who has failed to take his knowledge beyond a very surface understanding of the details presented.

MAIN USE
The main use of each statement is in most cases self-evident and these have each been discussed in detail in preceding chapters. However, they are summarized below to remind the reader and to emphasize the purpose of each statement.

SUPPLEMENTARY USE
Each statement has at least one supplementary use. Underlying every management technique whether it refers directly to finance or not, such as production control or marketing, is the purpose of improving the return on the capital employed. In addition to this use, there may well be further uses which help in interpreting and understanding the data.

We shall now examine the financial statements presented to management, taking into account these three points.

Balance Sheets and Profit and Loss Statements
These statements were dealt with in detail in Chapter 2.

LIMITATIONS
1 The valuation of items presented on the balance sheet is subject to varying interpretations as outlined earlier in this chapter, for example, fixed assets at cost, stock with or without the inclusion of all overheads. This leads to confusion in understanding and in certain cases great shock is experienced when the business is valued

for sale. It must always be noted that the balance sheet is constructed as it applies to a business as a going concern. This presupposes certain values which would be very different if the business were to be sold under an auctioneer's hammer. For example, work in progress, whatever is included in its cost, is assumed to be saleable whereas in the event of a business closing down, no one would pay much for partly produced manufactured items such as these. This practical limitation to the valuations set out in balance sheets must be carefully considered by all those viewing these statements.

2 The presentation of profit and loss statements is subject to the underlying influence of the theory of including all possible expenses and excluding all except certain income. This conservative attitude towards profit and loss presentation must be clearly understood when reading and interpreting revenue statements.

Those wishing to consider these limitations in the presentation of balance sheets and profit and loss statements should keep themselves informed by reading the financial press and by following the arguments and statements made by the accountancy profession.

3 The presentation of these final accounts is all based on historical data and therefore to use them as a basis for viewing the future can be misleading. This is especially true the farther away from the period under review the statements are prepared.

MAIN USE

The main use of these two statements is to review the return on the capital employed. These two fundamental financial questions, which were discussed in detail in Chapter 2, form the basis of all accounting information and are the genesis of all financial information systems.

SUPPLEMENTARY USES

1 A review of the data prepared in balance sheets and profit and loss statements over two or more periods enables the preparation of information regarding the flow of cash throughout the enterprise. Such cash-flow analysis can provide a most useful assessment as to the effectiveness of management's investment control.

2 The preparation of balance sheets and profit and loss statements presupposes a system of data-recording which in itself creates records of real management value. For instance, a detailed account of liquid resources in the form of a cash and bank account will be kept together with records of amounts due to and from individual customers. These latter data will enable managers to formulate and carry through an effective system of credit control which will reduce the capital tied up in working capital.

3 The regular flow of balance sheet and profit and loss statements

highlights the management need to invest capital and earn an adequate return for the investor. This financial purpose of business investment is given emphasis by these two statements and the maximization of return on capital employed will only be obtained if all managers are first aware of the problems involved and, second, can relate the financial data presented to this problem.

Full Costing

The preparation of full costing data is dealt with in Chapter 3.

LIMITATIONS

1 As in the case of balance sheets, the major limitation to costing data is in the basis of valuation. A cost is an analysis of expenses and income which have been incurred and received by the business and if this analysis is exact the values used will be in accordance with this actual income and expense. For this reason, if the costs have altered since the date of compilation, it will mean that the costing data prepared will be irrelevant if used to determine present or future costs. It is, therefore, very important to question most carefully the basis of arriving at each cost to see that it fulfils the needs of those requiring the cost. For example, a manager seeking to determine whether a particular product will give the business a reasonable profit based on a particular sales price needs to have a cost produced reflecting future rather than historical costs.

2 A further limitation to costing data lies in the fact that all indirect expenses added to the costs will be calculated on guesses which require to be checked against current data before their accuracy can be verified. This problem, referred to in detail in Chapter 3, makes it most important for costing data which include such expenses to be treated as pending confirmation before action is taken based upon them.

MAIN USES

1 The major use of costing data is to analyse the profit and losses of the enterprise under each product, service or activity. This analysis calls for a clear definition of need by the management of the business and all managers should concern themselves with the problem of defining what is termed "the cost units".

2 The analysis of expenses and income into cost units also enables these items to be related to areas of management and geographical control known as "cost centres". This provides useful control data for the business which can assist in making managers aware of their financial responsibilities.

1 The way in which expenses and income are analysed for costing purposes provides data for both estimating and budgeting purposes. Once a costing system has been introduced a mass of data will be collected on both expenses and income and this will prove invaluable in establishing estimates of product costs to be produced in future periods and also in setting up forecasting information for budgetary-control purposes.

2 A further indirect use of costing is that it assists in analysing the return on the capital employed. This is the underlying reason for this technique and although it is listed as a supplementary use, it is placed in this category only because once costing has been introduced, the product, service or activity analysis becomes the technique's concern. However, it should never be forgotten that this analysis is all created in order to investigate the return on the capital employed.

3 The needs for expense/revenue analysis are so frequent that it is beyond the scope of this chapter to set out each one in detail. Nevertheless, whenever such analysis takes place, it will be based upon a costing system. For example, the determination of the cost of hiring as opposed to running one's own transport fleet, the choice of whether to use a marketing consultant or to employ such expertise within one's own enterprise are just two examples of the analysis problems in which a costing system can give assistance.

Marginal Costing

The system is set out in detail in Chapter 3.

1 The first limitation of this technique is identical to that outlined for full costing, namely, valuation. In the same way marginal costs will be built up based on historical expense and income data available which may be out of date at the time of presentation.

2 As indirect expenses are in most cases fixed expenses these will not need to be included in the marginal costs. For this reason the volume of guesses required to charge such expenses to the unit costs will not be wanted. However, some variable costs may be indirect and these will need to be forecast as explained previously.

3 The adoption of this costing system is possible only where the variable expenses form a reasonable proportion of the total costs. When this proportion falls below 50 per cent the contribution shown will be so large that it will be difficult to form any real impression as to products' profitability.

4 The last limitation, which was dealt with in detail in Chapter 3, concerns the level of production or output of the enterprise. Such limitations are inherent in the data in that it is assumed in the definition of expenses being either fixed or variable that the level of output will never be less nor more than a given quantity. The transient nature of this classification of fixed and variable expenses must be noted by all managers so that marginal cost information can be read with a due recognition of this limitation.

MAIN USES
1 The main use of marginal costing is to analyse income and expenses in such a manner as to assist managers' understanding and control of the factors affecting profits. Within this area of management understanding can be classed the determination of the break-even point, the contribution per limiting factor and product profitability comparisons. All these uses have been dealt with earlier.

2 Together with these major uses can be added the way of examining unit marginal costs so as to determine sales prices in periods of fierce competition or when production capacity well exceeds the sales volume of units.

SUPPLEMENTARY USE

The general beneficial effect of educating managers into recognizing variable as opposed to fixed costs cannot be too strongly emphasized. It will concentrate managers' attention on those areas in which their control will be most effective. Their understanding of the fact that no profits can be made before period or fixed expenses have been recovered and that profit in relation to the limiting factor is the real profit measure will create a much more financially aware management team and will assist in the maximization of return on capital employed.

Budgetary Control

This information system is discussed in detail in Chapter 4.

LIMITATIONS

1 Once again, the limitation of this information technique is that the budget data may well change. It is important to keep the values continually under review so that managers concerned with budget comparison are aware of any changes, and explanations are given of the effect of such variations.

2 The limitation of this technique will be increased or reduced by the organization of the system. Both the preparation and progressing

of budgets must be such as to facilitate the best possible management control.

1 A budget presupposes a setting up of targets for all financial transactions. This will entail much investigation and examination on the part of managers of the expenses and income within their control. This will have a most salutary effect upon all those concerned. The first use of budgetary control is in the establishment of budgets entailing a full review of all expenses, income and investment, and the provision of the necessary capital for these purposes.

2 The second use of this technique is to compare such budgets with the actual financial transactions as they take place. Such comparison will highlight variations and these will call for interpretation which will in its turn demand management involvement. This second stage of comparison and analysis might be termed "management by objectives" in financial terms.

SUPPLEMENTARY USE
The major supplementary use of budgetary control is the discipline it provides the enterprise. In the first instance the technique presupposes a corporate policy. Without a policy budgetary control is impossible. The second discipline is seen in the preparation of individual budgets for each manager and their comparison against actual performance. This second step gives managers an understanding of their contribution towards the financial control of the business. This technique again emphasizes the financial objective, namely the maximizing of the return on capital invested.

Standard Costing

This technique was dealt with in detail in Chapter 5.

LIMITATIONS
The limitations listed under "Budgetary Control" apply equally to standard costing and these again were discussed earlier in the text. However, there is a further limitation in the case of this technique and that is the volume of data necessary as a prerequisite to its introduction. Many data are required for the successful introduction of budgetary control but standard costing requires considerably more data for a satisfactory analysis of the differences under their several causes. For this reason, it is most important for managers to consider carefully their needs for such analysis and limit

them as much as possible so as to reduce the clerical effort required to implement this technique.

The main use of standard costing is to pinpoint the cause of differences between standards for income and expenses and the actual performance. By isolating differences managers are able to take appropriate action to avoid those that are adverse and make permanent those that are favourable.

SUPPLEMENTARY USES
1 Standard costing presupposes the setting up of standards in such a way that differences of significance can be extracted. For this to happen the standards must be based on careful observations, studies and forecasts of the income and expenses involved. This, in many cases, leads to standards being set up which have more than one use. For example, labour standards can be used for wage incentive schemes, and material standards can be used to assist the material control aspect of production control.

2 A further use of this technique is that once standards have been set up it is possible to produce estimates for products with greater accuracy.

3 Finally, standard costing used throughout the concern will lead to the adoption of the technique of management by exception for the financial transactions concerned. It will make it possible for managers to concentrate their attention on areas of difference from standard and this should provide more time for managers to undertake their duties effectively.

Fixed-asset Appraisal

These techniques were described in detail in Chapter 6.

LIMITATION
The limitation of the data provided by this technique is that it is all based on forecasts or estimates of the cash flow and investment cost and these must be closely progressed over the periods ahead. Circumstances can arise to make all the forecasts incorrect and the limitation of the forecast can never be over-emphasized.

MAIN USES
1 The use of this technique is to determine as far as possible whether or not to invest the capital of the business in particular fixed assets.

2 A second use is to point out to all managers their responsibility

for investment under this head. This responsibility is just as applicable to an office manager installing a piece of office equipment as for a plant manager proposing to purchase a particular machine tool.

SUPPLEMENTARY USES
1 The introduction of fixed-asset appraisal requires the prior introduction of capital expenditure budgeting and the presetting of the criteria rates of return or payback to be adopted, for example, the number of years in which payback will be required and/or the rate of return needed if the D.C.F. method is adopted. This preliminary discipline will be found to have a beneficial effect upon the enterprise and this will also be true for the data which must be stored in order to create a system of investment appraisal. Such data will include an analysis of fixed assets, life expectations under their several categories and the net cash flow estimated for particular items.

2 Once again, a supplementary use of this technique will be to highlight the need to obtain an adequate return on the capital invested.

Working-Capital Analysis

This technique is dealt with in Chapter 6.

LIMITATIONS
1 The technique is based on forecasts for each working capital item in relation to a particular sales volume for a particular period. For this reason the technique is limited by the accuracy of the forecasts.

2 The values given to each item may be found to be incorrect and this may significantly affect the use of this technique.

MAIN USE
Working-capital analysis discovers the amount of working capital required for different levels of turnover, thus providing managers with a yardstick to assess the working-capital needs in the case of increasing or reducing activity.

SUPPLEMENTARY USES
1 Perhaps the greatest supplementary use of this technique is the understanding the technique gives to all managers of their interdependence one with the other in this area of financial investment. This is true of all areas of financial control, but this particular technique is especially relevant here.

2 The second supplementary use of this technique is again in the

field of management education and shows the connection between time and money. The amount of working capital required per amount of sales will be controlled by time and throughout the analysis time is found to be capital. The understanding of the connection of time and money is essential to all financial interpretation and this point is very forcibly set out in this area of analysis.

3 Finally, this technique once again illustrates the nature of business investment and the need to maximize return on the capital invested.

INTERPRETATION OF FINANCIAL INFORMATION

In this examination of financial information a common use of all the data has been found—the interpretation of return on capital investment. At the beginning of this book financial information was introduced as providing for the basic needs of all investors, first, to know what return was being earned on the capital invested, and, second, to know exactly where the investment had been made. From these needs all the supplementary information techniques have been developed and these in their turn are designed to amplify and thus give more information regarding these two fundamental questions.

The interpretation of all financial data must be based upon a real understanding of the information. This will necessitate knowing exactly what is being presented, how the data have been compiled, what can be learned from them and recognizing both the limitations and the uses of the information.

Ratio Analysis

Once this basic knowledge has been established, it is possible to use the interpretation technique known as ratio analysis.

This technique is one which grows with use and understanding and is simply an examination of data by means of expressing items as percentages or ratios of other items, so as to examine investment and trading performance. It is usually found that ratios are of little value unless traced over a series of periods so as to produce trends.

RATIO TREND

The use of trend examination is the most common application of ratio analysis and in fact it is difficult to find any ratio which, examined in isolation, can be found significant. Trend examination may be based on the results of a business over present and past periods or

167

present, past and future periods. Such examination will indicate how performance is progressing within the particular business. However, to assess the standing of a business in the context of its particular industry it is more valuable to compare its ratios with those which exist in businesses similar to its own. This form of outside comparison is facilitated by the data made available by Interfirm Comparison Ltd. Full details of this organization and the literature it publishes are available from its offices at Management House, Parker Street, London, WC2B 5PT.

RATIO ANALYSIS OF FINANCIAL DATA

We shall now examine the summarized profit and loss statements and balance sheets of a business over the last four years.

SUMMARIZED PROFIT & LOSS STATEMENTS

		1970 £000	1969 £000	1968 £000	1967 £000
Sales	(A)	10,000	8,000	6,500	6,000
Materials		4,000	3,000	2,500	2,200
Labour		2,000	1,800	1,500	1,300
Production Costs . . .	(B)	6,000	4,800	4,000	3,500
Gross Profit . . .	(A − B) (C)	4,000	3,200	2,500	2,500
Investment Income		1,000	800	800	800
	(D)	5,000	4,000	3,300	3,300
Administrative Expenses . . .		1,600	1,200	1,000	1,000
Financial Expenses		100	120	80	100
Selling Expenses		1,900	1,500	1,690	1,260
	(E)	3,600	2,820	2,770	2,360
NET PROFIT (D − E). . . .		1,400	1,180	530	940

In the data summarized above and on page 171 it will be noted that taxation has been excluded together with interest and dividend payments. The reason for these omissions will be explained when we examine the results set out in the following paragraphs.

Return on Capital Employed

The first point of examination in these two statements will be the return on capital employed. In this examination capital employed will be taken to include share capital, reserves—excluding those for

SUMMARIZED BALANCE SHEETS

	1970 £000	1969 £000	1968 £000	1967 £000
FROM WHERE CAPITAL OBTAINED				
Share Capital . . .	3,000	2,500	2,000	2,000
Reserves	625	508	705	1,040
Long-term loans . .	500	500	500	500
CAPITAL EMPLOYED . .	£4,125	3,508	3,205	3,540
FIXED ASSETS				
Property	2,000	1,600	1,500	1,700
Plant and Machinery . .	1,500	1,400	1,300	1,400
Office Equipment . .	500	400	300	300
	4,000	3,400	3,100	3,400
INVESTMENTS . . .	100	80	80	80
	4,100	3,480	3,180	3,480

		1970	1969	1968	1967
WORKING CAPITAL					
CURRENT ASSETS					
Stock . . .	100		60	70	90
Debtors . .	70		70	51	70
Cash . . .	5		8	4	10
	175		138	125	170
Less: CURRENT LIABILITIES					
Creditors . . .	150		110	100	110
	25		28	25	60
		4,125	3,508	3,205	3,540

taxation—long-term loans and bank overdraft. This definition of capital employed is one which is largely accepted although several other versions are in current use. The limitation of this figure already referred to in this chapter and relating to the underlying values of the assets and current liabilities must be considered as this may have a very significant effect upon the ratio of return to this figure.

The return figure will be the net profit excluding taxation and interest on capital. Taxation is omitted as it is considered that the amount of this item may vary from year to year for reasons outside the trading ability of the organization. For example, the large capital allowances available to a business in the early years of their purchase will reduce the tax deduction. This reason for excluding taxation as a charge owing to its varying nature might lead someone examining profits in this connection to omit any other non-recurring or exceptional item of expense or income. This would more likely create data of a comparable nature from year to year.

The omission of interest is so as to arrive at a measure of return against capital employed and if this exclusion did not take place it would be measuring a return *after* a return had been obtained. From these data the return on capital employed before interest and taxation is as follows:

$$1967 = 27 \text{ per cent}$$
$$1968 = 17 \text{ ,, ,,}$$
$$1969 = 34 \text{ ,, ,,}$$
$$1970 = 34 \text{ ,, ,,}$$

These percentages show an uneven trend over the first three years which flattens out in the last two years.

Further investigation can take place in two areas:

(i) the relationship of profits to sales; and
(ii) the use of capital and therefore the investment of the enterprise.

It will therefore be the next stage in the examination to investigate under these two heads. In this examination we shall concentrate upon operating profits and operating assets. This will require the exclusion of expenses, income and investment which does not relate to the trading activities of the enterprise. For this purpose the data in the illustration have been adjusted as follows:

NET PROFIT/LOSS

	1970 £000	1969 £000	1968 £000	1967 £000
Profits as per illustration . . .	1,400	1,180	530	940
Less: Investment income . . .	1,000	800	800	800
	400	380	−270	140
Add/Less: Financial expenses . .	100	120	80	100
Adjusted net profit	500	500	−190	240

OPERATING ASSETS

	1970 £000	1969 £000	1968 £000	1967 £000
Capital employed	4,125	3,508	3,205	3,540
Less: Investment	100	80	80	80
Operating assets	4,025	3,428	3,125	3,460

The Relationship of Profit to Sales

The ratios which relate to the relationship between profit and sales begin with the overall assessment of trading profit to sales and this is then analysed into its component parts. This can be illustrated by the following diagram:

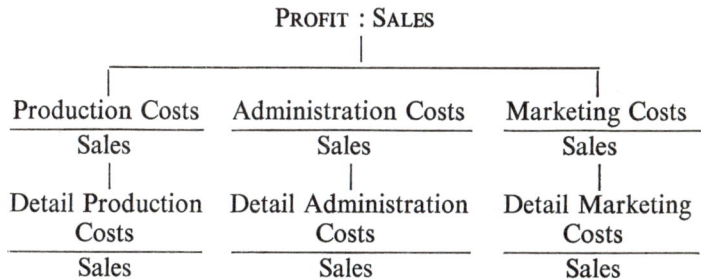

PROFIT : SALES

Production Costs	Administration Costs	Marketing Costs
Sales	Sales	Sales

Detail Production Costs	Detail Administration Costs	Detail Marketing Costs
Sales	Sales	Sales

These ratios can be illustrated from the data presented in the example as follows:

	1970 %	1969 %	1968 %	1967 %
Profit to sales	5·0	6·25	−2·90	4·0
Production costs	60·0	60·0	61·6	58·3
Administration costs	16·0	15·0	15·4	16·6
Selling costs	19·0	18·75	26·0	21·0

It will be noted that the profits which are examined in this further analysis are those relating to the trading operations of the enterprise and as such exclude financial expenses and investment interest.

The Use of Assets

The assets which will be used in this examination will be what are termed the "operating assets" such as fixed assets and working capital and will exclude investment outside the business. The investigation will take the form of relating sales to these assets both in total and in detail. By this means it will be possible to trace the number of times margins are made during the period under examination. For example, in 1970 the profit margin to sales is 4·0 and the sales to operating assets are 1·70. If we multiply 4·0 by 1·7 we arrive at 6·8 which is the rate of operating profits to operating assets in 1970. The following diagram illustrates how the sales to operating assets ratios relate one to the other

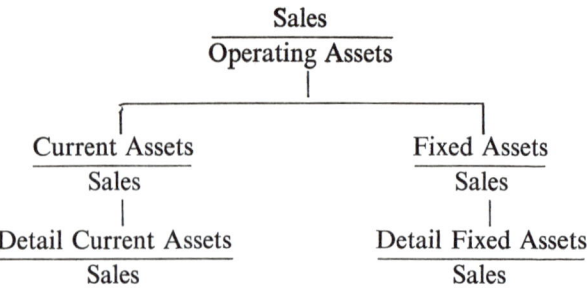

$$\frac{\text{Sales}}{\text{Operating Assets}}$$

$$\frac{\text{Current Assets}}{\text{Sales}} \qquad \frac{\text{Fixed Assets}}{\text{Sales}}$$

$$\frac{\text{Detail Current Assets}}{\text{Sales}} \qquad \frac{\text{Detail Fixed Assets}}{\text{Sales}}$$

We shall now examine these ratios from the data presented in the previous illustration.

	1970	1969	1968	1967
Operating Assets:				
Sales	2·4	2·3	2·8	1·7
Current Assets:				
Sales	57·0	58·0	52·0	35·0
Fixed Assets:				
Sales	2·5	2·4	2·1	1·8

The Provision of Funds

We have so far examined the operating performance of the enterprise. It may also be useful to investigate its financial stability or otherwise and this will require ratios summarizing this aspect of the data. In the investigation we should examine the trend of borrowing, the safety of such borrowing, the position of the current liabilities, the liquidity of funds, etc.

We shall express this examination in the terms of the illustration. For this purpose we will first view the trend of obtaining funds over the past four years, as follows:

	1970	1969	1968	1967
As a Percentage of Total Capital Employed				
Share Capital	72·6	71·3	62·4	56·4
Reserves	15·3	14·5	22·0	29·5
Long-term Loans	12·1	14·2	15·6	14·1

The position of temporary finance can be examined as follows:

	1970	1969	1968	1967
Current Assets to Current Liabilities	1·17	1·25	1·25	1·45

172

This overall cover ratio which proves that current liabilities, i.e creditors, are covered by those assets which will become cash, might be expanded as follows:

	1970	1969	1968	1967
DEBTORS AND CASH TO CURRENT LIABILITIES	0·5	0·7	0·55	0·7

This gives a quick or real liquid test as to the ability to meet debts immediately and highlights any trend towards a business becoming less liquid.

USE OF RATIOS

Having presented the ratios, it is necessary to use them to examine and investigate the business. Such an examination might take place in the following stages:

STAGE

1 Profit to Capital Employed ratio down in trend.
2 Why?
3 Profit to Sales lower than previous years.
4 Why?
5 Marketing Costs to Sales increase.
6 Why?
7 Commission Rate to Salesmen increased during present year.
8 Why?
9 In accordance with decision at directors' meeting to help increase sales of new product.

From this example it can be seen that ratio analysis leads to a logical flow of questions and answers until the reason is isolated and the cause located. It may be found that ratio analysis leads to further investigation outside the data under examination. For example, if labour costs are found to be increasing, it may lead to an investigation of the costing system and the work-study system. Again, if sales divided by plant and machinery show a reduction in the turnover times, this might lead to an investigation of the fixed-asset appraisal techniques in use.

Ratios are a beginning to investigation and not the end. They provide a logical basis for investigation and as such should be treated with care both in their preparation and use.

CONCLUSION

Interpretation of financial data is the final stage in the understanding of financial technique. Too often the manager tries to interpret before understanding the underlying data. It is tempting to reach for ratios without understanding the data from which they have been produced and therefore not understanding their limitations as well as their uses.

Interpretation must begin from an understanding of the financial techniques which have been discussed in previous chapters. It is a technique which will expand with understanding and practice. The manager must learn to ask questions about the data until he is fully satisfied that he understands the answers. He must trace the logic of each ratio used to interpret the data and see how one answer complements another. It is at this stage of interpretation that freedom from jargon is essential if real understanding is to exist, and those presenting financial data must realize that they are providing a service that is both required and used by management.

It is up to all managers to insist that the data should be presented in a logical and clear manner so that the maximum use can be made of it in managing the enterprise. This is just another example of maximizing the return on the capital investment!

Annotated Reading List

The following list of books is not a comprehensive bibliography but is intended to provide guidance on further reading.

A. General Texts on the Scope and Application of Financial Accounting

1. Burke, W. L., and Smyth, E. B., *Accounting for Management* (Sydney, Australia: The Law Book Company Limited, 1966, 514 pp.)

   Deals generally with the way in which accounting methods assist management and emphasizes the services expected of the accountant in providing data required by management for planning, solving problems, making investment and other decisions, exacting responsibility, and measuring the performance of people at all levels.

2. Lynch, R. M., *Accounting for Management* (New York: McGraw-Hill Book Company, 1967, 447 pp.)

   An introduction to the usefulness of accounting for informing management decisions in planning and control.

3. Murphy, Mary E., *Managerial Accounting* (Princeton, NJ: D. Van Nostrand Co., 1963, 276 pp.)

   Deals generally with the use of accounting data for managerial decision. Intended as an introduction to the idea of functional participation by accounting in general management.

4. Sizer, John, *An Insight into Management Accounting* (Pelican Library of Business and Management, 1969, 341 pp.)

   A general survey of financial information which is intended for the manager with no basic accounting knowledge.

   The book is well illustrated and designed to give the reader an understanding of current management accounting practice.

5. Smith, R. L., *Management through Accounting* (NJ: Prentice Hall, 1962, 457 pp.)

    Introduces the various managerial processes as problems and suggests means of solving them.

B. An Introduction to Accounting Itself for Those without Formal Training in Accountancy

6. Bull, R. J., *Accounting in Business* (Butterworths, 1969, 248 pp.)

    Accounting concepts simply presented with the idea of discovering principles and providing a broad perspective of business accounting.

7. Duck, R. E. V., and Jervis, F. R. J., *Management Accounting* (Harrap, 1964, 303 pp.)

    Assuming no previous knowledge of the subject, explains the meaning of accounts and their use in assisting management.

8. Hartley, W. C. F., *An Introduction to Business Accounting for Managers* (Pergamon, 1966, 160 pp.)

    Provides a general appreciation of the principles and technique of accounting and of the use and limitations of the accounting service; for those who are taking a course in business or management studies.

9. Kohler, E. L., *Accounting for Management* (NJ: Prentice Hall, 1965, 275 pp.)

    Sets out the principal features of accounting without recourse to model book-keeping and problem solving. It is intended for executives at all levels who have to deal with accounting and accountants.

10. Robson, A. P., *Essential Accounting for Managers* (Cassell, 1966, 132 pp.)

    Gives short explanations of accounting principles and techniques and provides a simple introduction for non-accountants.

11. Waldron, R. S., *Understanding Accounts* (Nelson, 1965, 123 pp.)

    For those starting to study management accounting methods, business control and organization.

12. Wood, F., *Business Accounting* I & II (Longmans, 1967, 1968, 779 pp.)

    These two books, which form a complete textbook on business accounting, seek to stress why as well as how financial information is produced.

C. Textbooks for Those Wishing to Extend Their Basic Knowledge

13. Batty, J., *Management Accountancy* (Macdonald & Evans, 2nd ed., 1966, 772 pp.)
    A standard textbook.

14. Bierman, H., and Drebin, A. R., *Managerial Accounting: An Introduction* (New York: Macmillan Company, 1968, 414 pp.)
    A detailed discussion of the preparation and utilization of financial information for purposes of internal management. Some previous knowledge is assumed of the principles of financial accounting and the basic accounting process.

15. Burney, A. G. B., *Illustrations of Management Accounts in Practice* (Gee, 1959, 126 pp.)
    A description and explanation of the managing accounting statements prepared for a small engineering concern.

16. Fertig, P. E., Istvan, D. F., and Mottice, H. J., *Using Accounting Information* (New York: Harcourt, Brace & World, 1965, 591 pp.)
    Deals with the uses of accounting information for decision-making inside and outside a business firm.

17. Gordon, M. J., and Shillinglaw, G., *Accounting: A Management Approach* (Richard D. Irwin, 3rd ed., 1964, 865 pp.)
    An introductory textbook which includes the management uses of internal accounting for planning and control and for the evaluation of alternative pricing, investment and other decisions.

18. Thornton, N., *Financial Information for Executive Management* (Gee, 1967, 180 pp.)
    Describes the methods employed by accountants to communicate financial information and contains practical illustrations of accounting reports applicable to many types of business.

D. Specialist Books on Management Control

19. Dearden, J., and McFarlan, F. W., *Management Information Systems: text and cases* (Richard D. Irwin, 1966, 427 pp.)
    Provides for students of business management an understanding of how the computer may be used as a managerial information tool. A prior knowledge is assumed of the technical aspects of data processing.

20. McDonough, A. M., and Garrett, L. J., *Management Systems* (Richard D. Irwin, 1965, 311 pp.)
    Deals with the development of an information system to serve the needs of top management. Systems design is treated

as a means for bringing together the best definitions of management problems and the best combination of personnel talents and systems techniques for handling these problems.

21. Rose, T. G., *Higher Control in Management* (Pitman, 7th ed., 1963, 281 pp.)

   This is a basic text on the subject of how financial information can best be presented to managers. The illustrations are still relevant today and form a very useful basis for those managers who wish to challenge the methods of presenting data.

E. Specialist Books on Investment Appraisal

22. Alfred, A. M., and Evans, J., *Appraisal of Investment Projects by Discounted Cash Flow* (Chapman & Hall, 1967, 71 pp.)

   A brief explanation of the principles with some shortcut techniques.

23. Bierman, H., Jr., and Smidt, S., *The Capital Budgeting Decision* (Collier-Macmillan International Editions, 1969, 420 pp.)

24. Merrett, A. J., and Sykes, A., *Capital Budgeting and Company Finance* (Longmans, 1966, 184 pp.)

   Covers the basic techniques of investment appraisal and gives an explanation of discounted cash flow. Also deals with matters of company finance and taxation.

25. Merrett, A. J., and Sykes, A., *The Finance and Analysis of Capital Projects*

   A standard work requiring some knowledge of mathematics and the basic principles of accounting. Of use to the non-specialist business executive as also to the specialist financial executive, accountant and business economist.

F. Other Texts

26. Coy, J., Clark, A. C., and Keens, S., *Accounting Case Studies* (Polytechnic Publishers, 1970, 151 pp.)

   This book contains a series of accounting case studies which are presented in a manner to assist those acquainted with financial data to use them for decision-making purposes.

27. Hofstede, G. H., *The Game of Budget Control* (Tavistock, 1968, 363 pp.)

   This book is the publication of a project carried out by the author into the budget-control systems of six manufacturing firms in the Netherlands. The research is primarily concerned with studying the human effects upon management of budgetary control and is of particular relevance to general management.

Index